和

The Wisdom of Ancient JAPAN

Timeless Lessons to Live By

Saori Okada

Michael O'Mara Books Limited

First published in Great Britain in 2025 by
Michael O'Mara Books Limited
9 Lion Yard, Tremadoc Road
London SW4 7NQ

EU representative:
Authorised Rep Compliance Ltd
Ground Floor, 71 Baggot Street Lower
Dublin D02 P593, Ireland

Text and illustrations copyright © Michael O'Mara Books Limited 2025

All rights reserved. You may not copy, store, distribute, transmit, reproduce or otherwise make available this publication (or any part of it) in any form, or by any means (electronic, digital, optical, mechanical, photocopying, recording, machine readable, text/data mining or otherwise), without the prior written permission of the publisher. Any person who does any unauthorized act in relation to this publication may be liable to criminal prosecution and civil claims for damages.

A CIP catalogue record for this book is available from the British Library.

This product is made of material from well-managed, FSC®-certified forests and other controlled sources. The manufacturing processes conform to the environmental regulations of the country of origin.

For further information about our green policy see
www.mombooks.com/about/sustainability-climate-focus
Report any safety issues to product.safety@mombooks.com

ISBN: 978-1-78929-824-6 in hardback print format

1 2 3 4 5 6 7 8 9 10

Cover designed by Natasha Le Coultre
Front cover image by Utagawa Hiroshige II, courtesy of Ashmolean Museum of Art and Archaeology/Heritage Images via Getty Images
Japanese calligraphy by Kyoko Okada, practising under the name 千彩 (Chisai)
Designed and typeset by Claire Cater
Printed and bound in China

www.mombooks.com

Introduction

In Japan, wisdom often lives quietly – tucked into daily rituals, shared through age-old phrases or felt in the turning of the seasons. These lessons aren't loud or grand but gentle, balanced and deeply human.

Having grown up in Japan, I've come to understand how these teachings – passed down across generations – shape not just how we live but how we connect, care and find meaning in the everyday.

This book is a collection of those gentle and powerful truths. From proverbs to cultural concepts, here, within the pages of this book, you will find sixty entries, each one inviting you to reflect and offering a small moment of reconnection – to yourself, to others and to what matters.

Let these pages be a soft place to land.
A space to pause, realign and remember the wisdom that already lives within you.

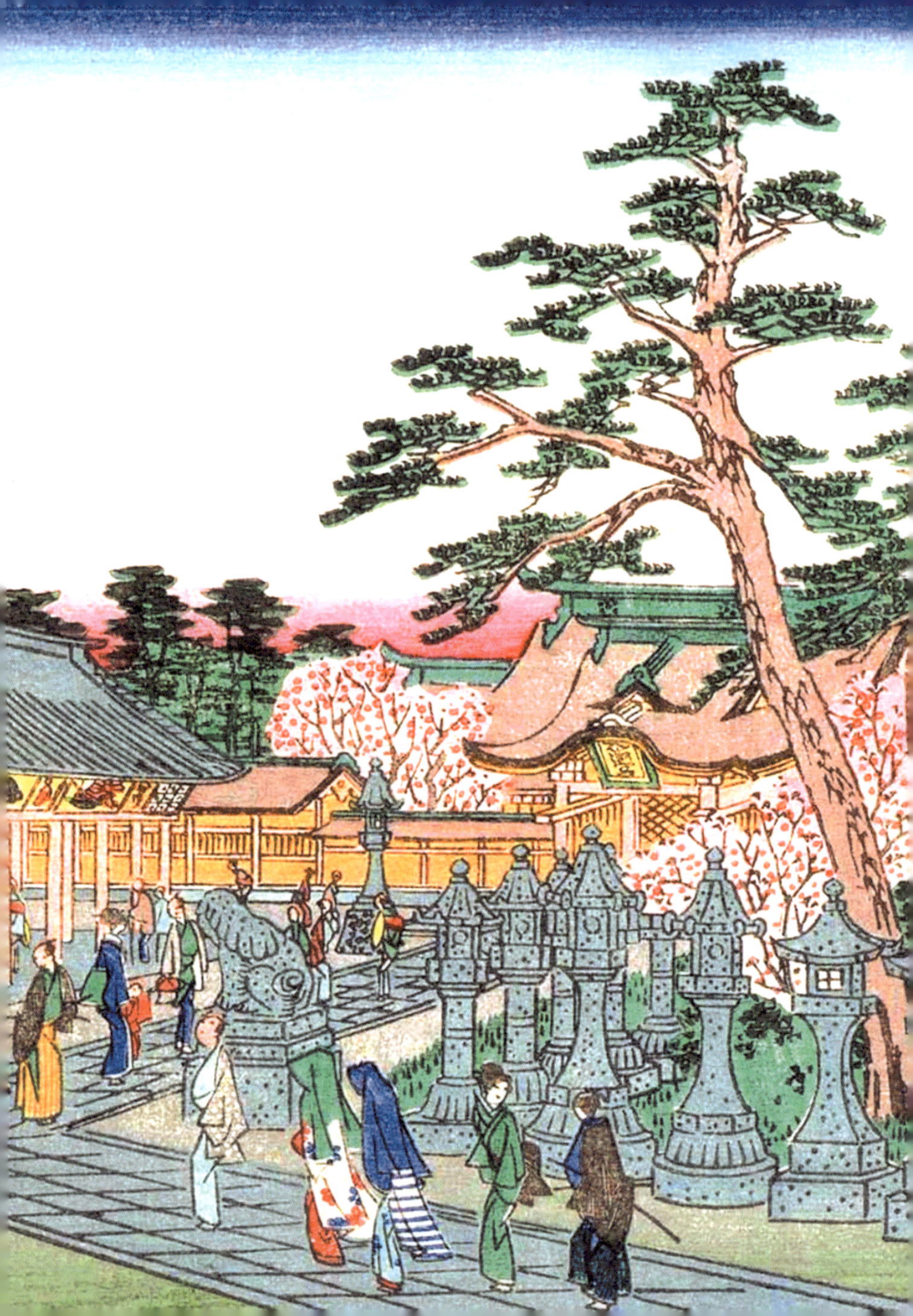

A-un

阿吽

Welcome the beginning and end of all things

A-un represents the first and last sound, the inhale and exhale, the beginning and end of the universe. Seen in pairs of temple guardian statues where one has its mouth open, 阿 (*a*), the other with its mouth closed, 吽 (*un*), *a-un* reflects the duality and cycle present in all things – light and shadow, stillness and movement, presence and absence. *A-un* embodies the synchronicity we experience when we move in harmony with these natural rhythms and embrace both beginnings and endings, knowing that life exists in the space between. Try a breathing exercise: take a deep breath in, and a deep breath out. Reflect on a recent beginning or ending. Breathe through this reflection without judgment – simply sit with yourself in stillness.

Ishin-denshin

以心伝心

Nurture soul-to-soul understanding

Ishin-denshin is the unspoken connection that flows directly from one heart to another. Rooted in Zen philosophy, it reminds us that true understanding does not always require words – some of the deepest connections are felt, not spoken. In moments of silence, we communicate through energy, intuition and sincerity. Reflect on the types of relationships where words are unnecessary: how do you cultivate this kind of understanding? Trust in the quiet language of the heart and let presence speak where words fall short.

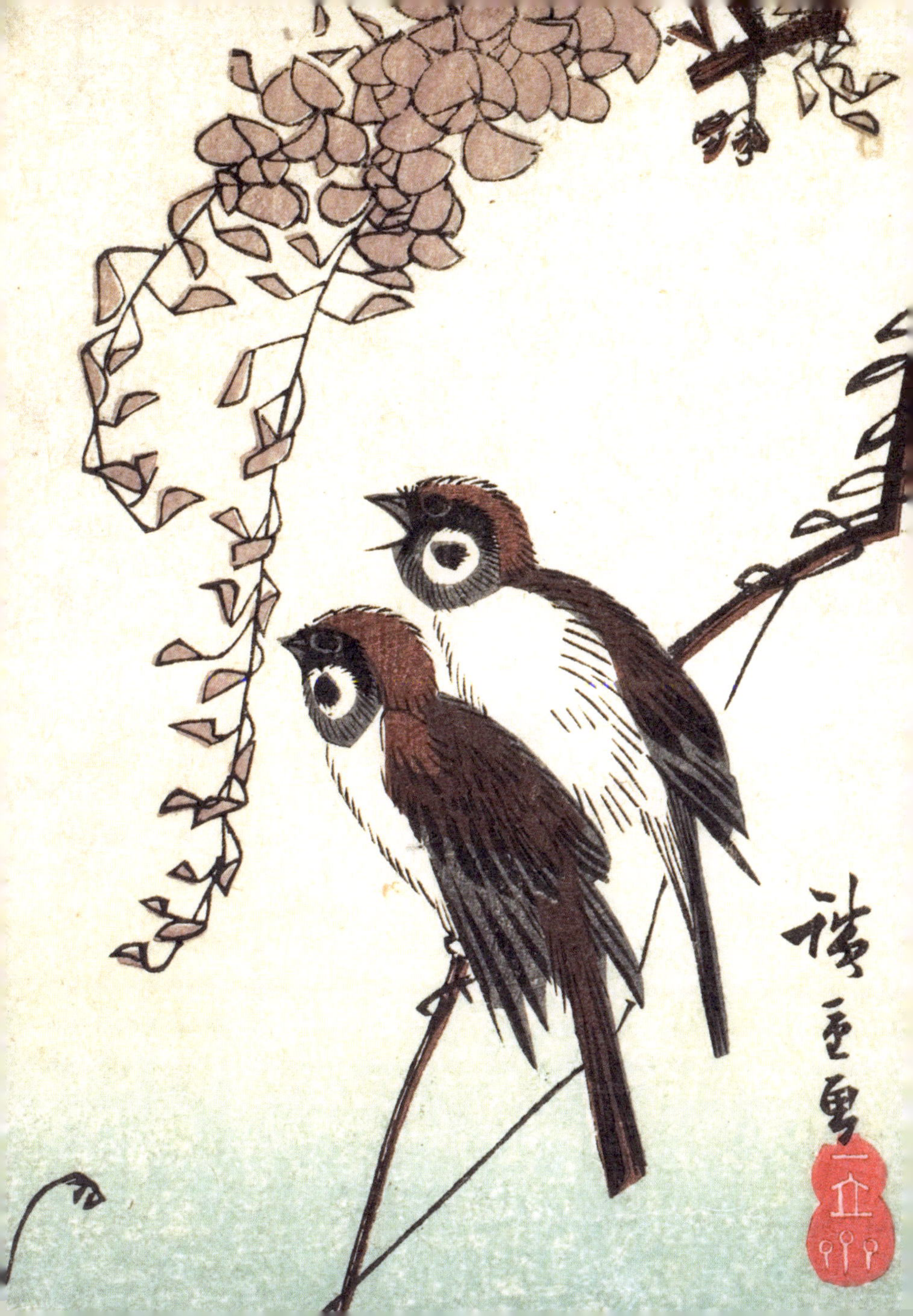

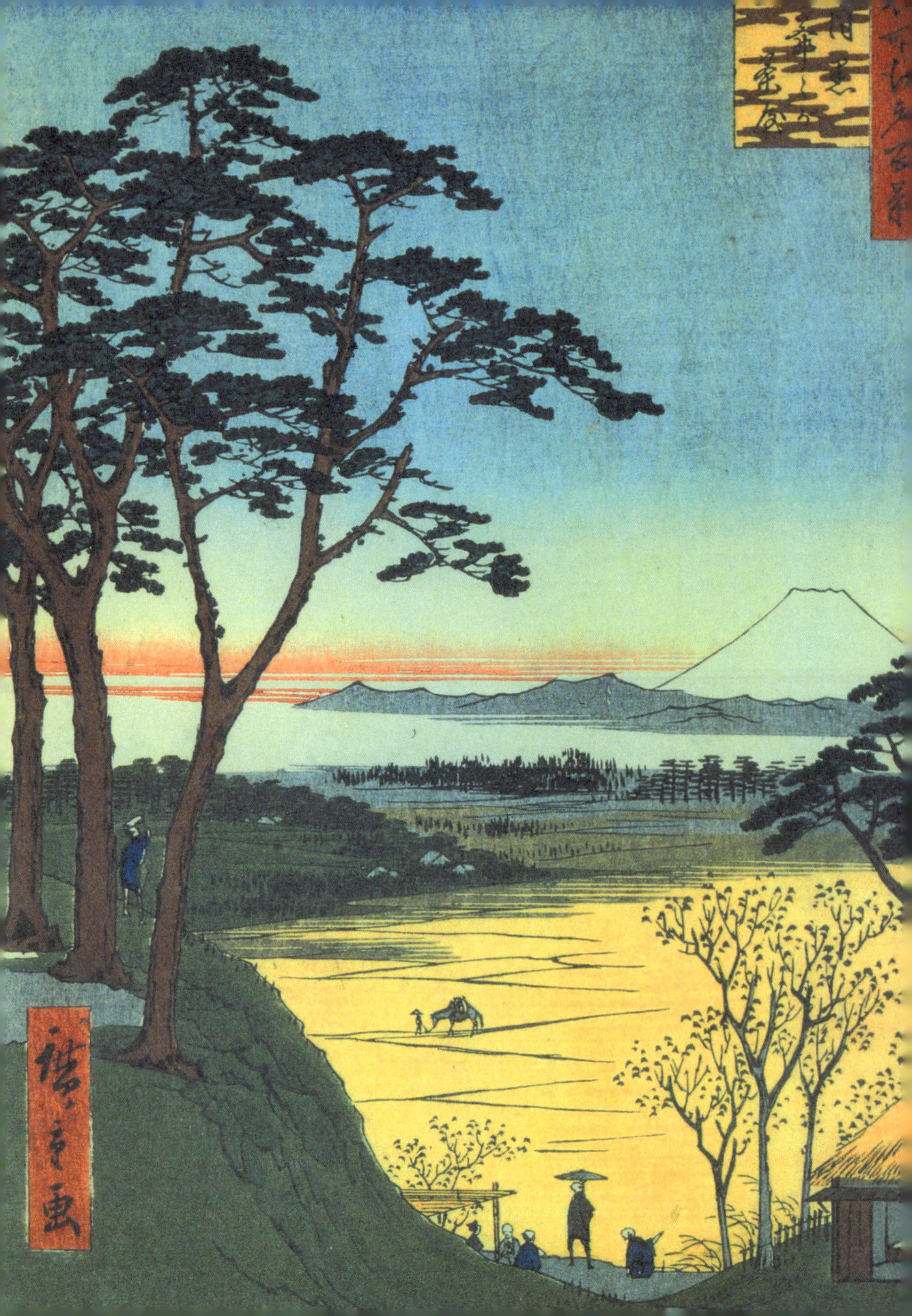
廣重画

Ibasho

居場所

Be where you belong

Ibasho is the space where one feels physically and emotionally at home. More than just a location, it represents the environments – within ourselves and through our connections with others – where we feel safe and free to be our authentic selves. *Ibasho* encourages us to seek relationships and surroundings that bring ease to the heart and nurture a deep sense of belonging. Reflect on the places and people that make you feel at home: do they support your authenticity and inner peace? Intentionally create these spaces to honour who you truly are.

Genki

元気

Check in with your foundational energy

Often translated as 'How are you?' in Japanese, *genki* carries a deeper meaning rooted in its characters, representing one's foundational energy. Check in with your *genki* to reconnect with the energy that sustains you, align with your soul and strengthen your foundation. Ask about the *genki* of others to foster meaningful connections and create moments of shared reflection on the energy that fuels us all. By recognizing the depth of *genki*, we deepen our awareness of the vital energy that fuels us all, cultivating kindness, authenticity and a greater sense of connection in daily life.

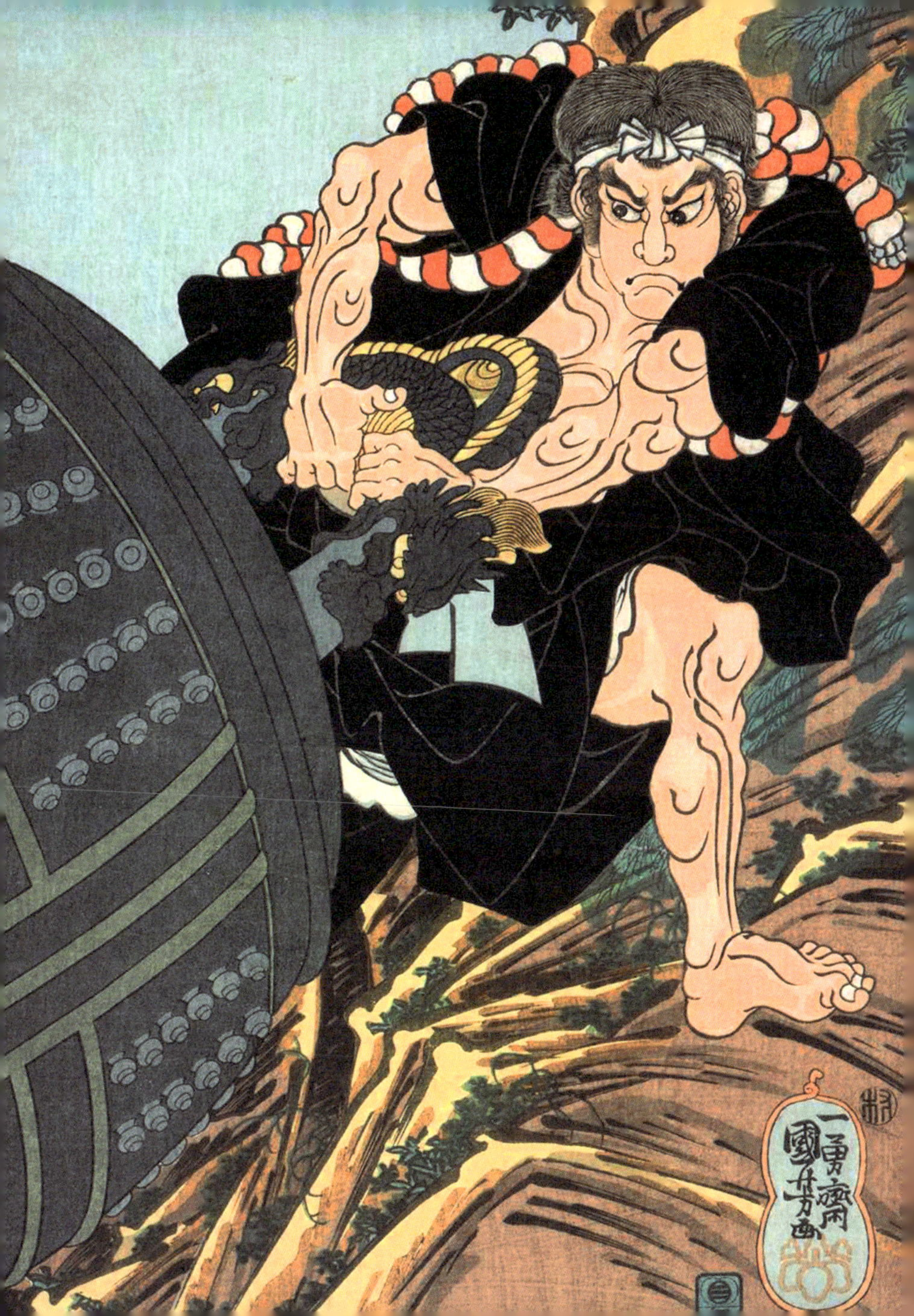
一勇齋
國芳画

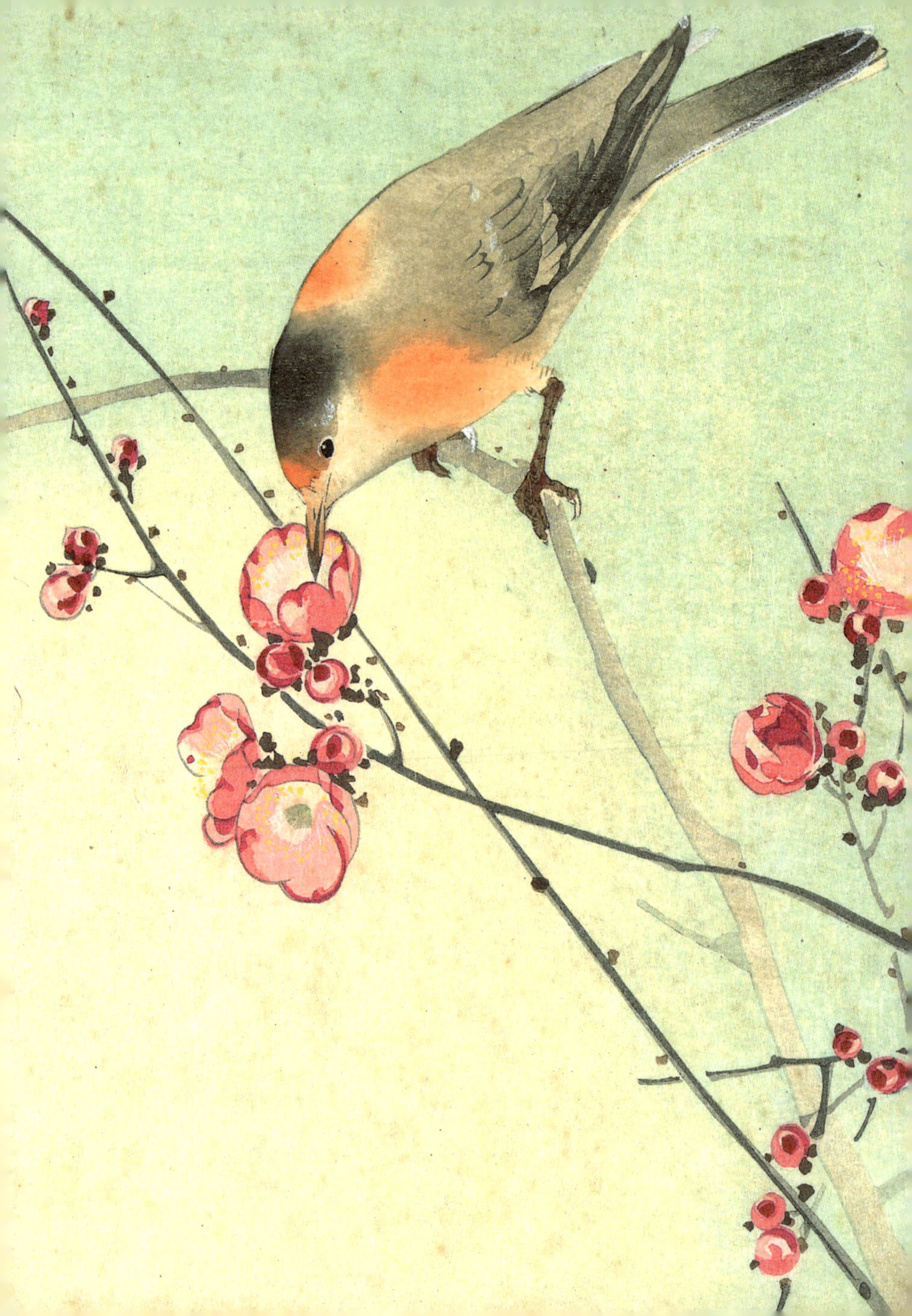

CONNECTION AND BELONGING

Arigatō

有難う

Gratitude is a precious gift

The Japanese word for thank-you carries a more profound meaning rooted in its characters, which represent 'difficult to have'. Connected to Buddhist thought, *arigatō* reflects the wisdom that being born as a human is itself a rare gift, and even more so, the kindness of others is something precious that we should never take for granted. By recognizing the intention behind saying thank-you, we cultivate a more meaningful appreciation for life's big and small moments. Let *arigatō* remind you to honour everyday moments of gratitude and strengthen your connection to others and the precious life we have been gifted.

Kotodama

言霊

Honour the spirit of words

Kotodama carries the wisdom that every word holds a spirit, shaping reality through energy. Words are not simply communication tools; they influence our thoughts, emotions and the world around us. Speak, write and share with intention, knowing that language has the power to transform lives, including your own. Honour words as a spiritual force by choosing them with care and discernment. Do your words build connection, inspire gratitude or bring authenticity? Use language as a gift to shape the world you wish to see.

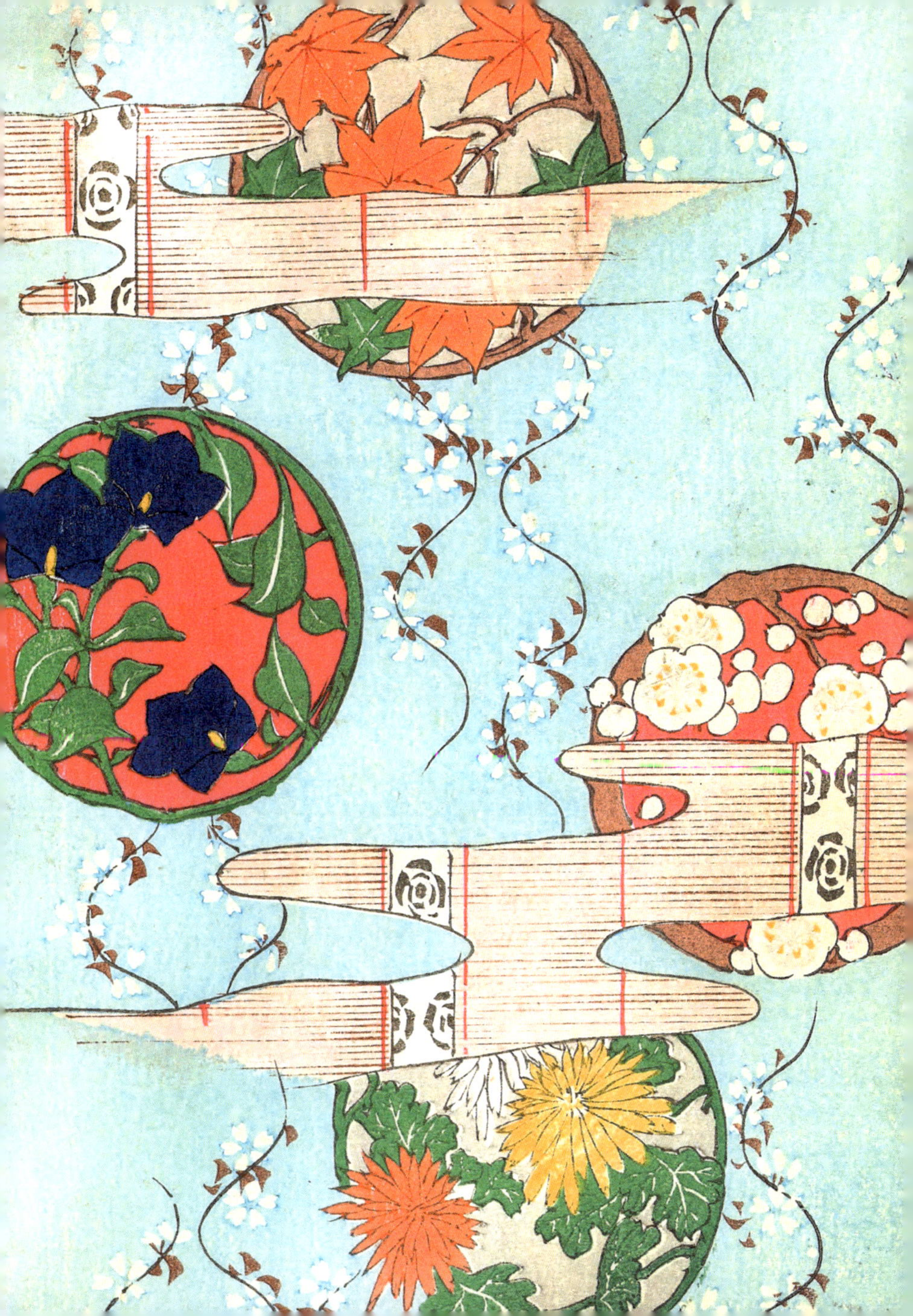

月耕隨筆

京名所　裏之高

CONNECTION AND BELONGING

Kizuna

絆

Lean into the invisible threads that strengthen us

Kizuna represents the unbreakable bonds that connect us, created through trust, shared experiences and moments that shape relationships over time. Like threads that grow stronger when woven together, our connections remind us of the power of unity. Let *kizuna* encourage you to lean into these bonds, knowing that true strength comes from recognizing we are not meant to walk alone. Reach out to someone you feel connected to. Send a message to check in, plan a catch-up walk, or simply express gratitude for their presence in your life. Nurture these relationships with care, as they empower you and those around you, strengthening the fabric of humanity.

Wa

和

Embrace the way of harmony

Wa embodies the spirit of peace, highlighting how individuals come together to support one another. Deeply ingrained in Japanese culture, *wa* symbolizes not only harmony but also Japan itself, reflecting a core value that has profoundly shaped society. *Wa* helps us see the quiet yet immense power of the collective, guiding us to choose unity over division and collaboration over personal gain. Look for a small way to support harmony in your community – perhaps by saying good morning to your neighbours, volunteering for a local cause, or offering a listening ear. Embrace the value of working together, fostering understanding and striving for harmony as a shared pursuit.

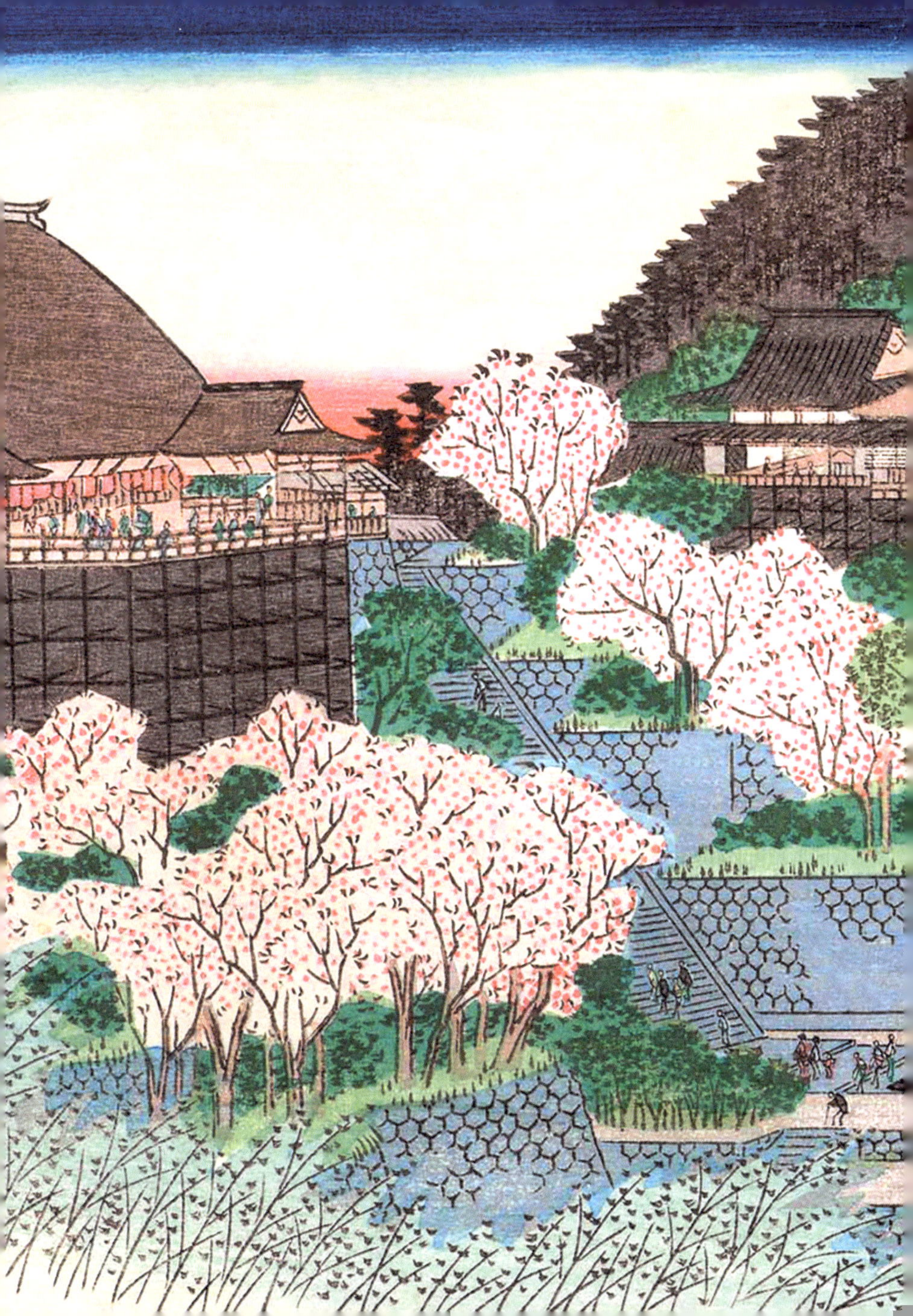

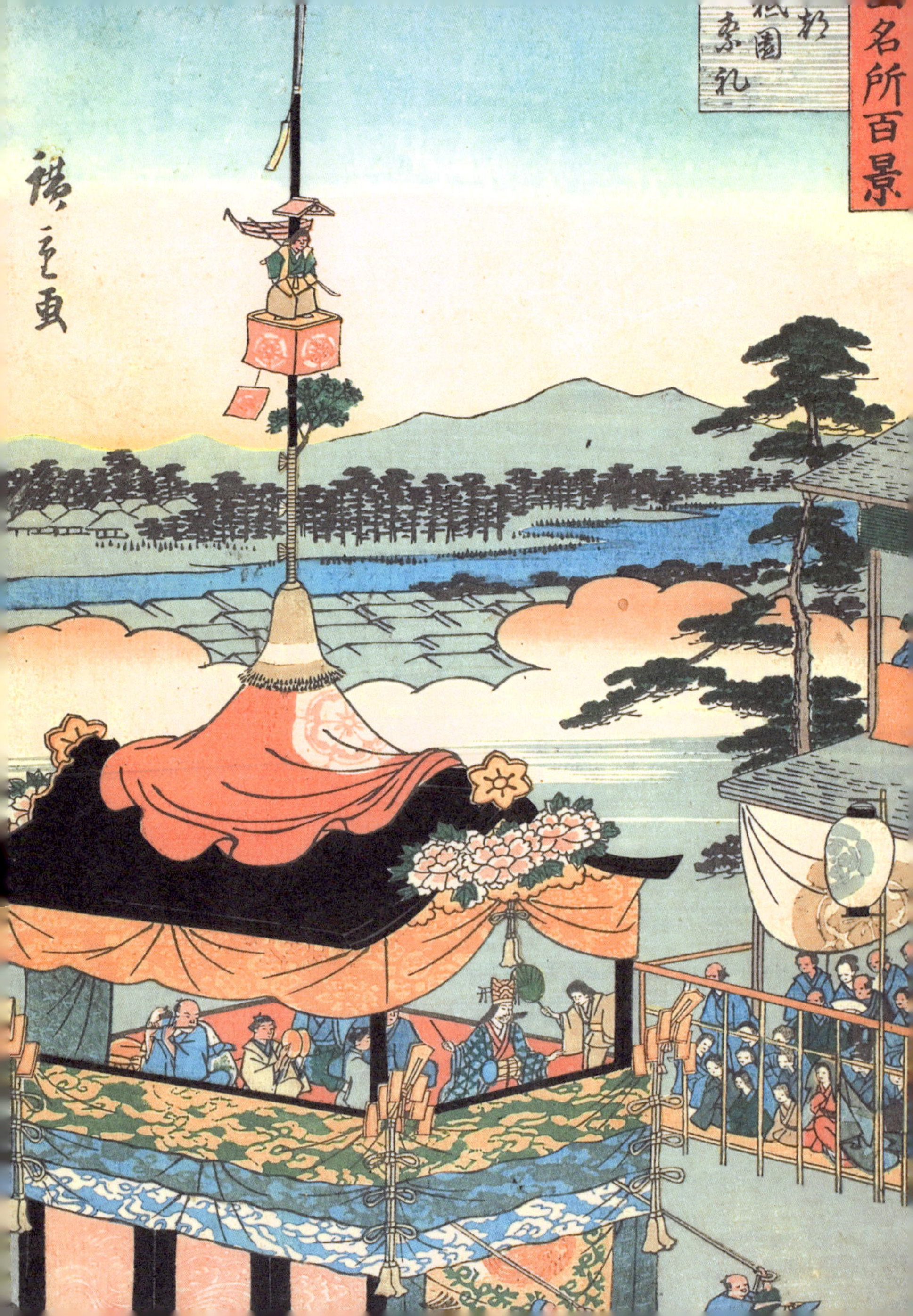
名所百景
都 祇園祭礼
廣重画

CONNECTION AND BELONGING

Go-en

ご縁

Trust the connections destiny brings your way

Life's connections often feel serendipitous – as if delicately guided by destiny. Though seemingly occurring by chance, these encounters have a deeper meaning, carrying the potential to teach, guide and empower us. *Go-en* reflects the wisdom that relationships and opportunities are not random but are part of the universe's interconnectedness. Celebrate the unexpected connections that have shaped your path and feel the *go-en* you have experienced in your past. Embrace future encounters with gratitude, knowing they hold the potential to play a profound role in your life.

CONNECTION AND BELONGING

Omotenashi

おもてなし

Offer wholehearted hospitality,
given without expectation

Omotenashi embodies a spirit of deep, sincere hospitality – an offering of care, attention and generosity without the expectation of something in return. Derived from おもて (*omote*, 'surface') and なし (*nashi*, 'none'), it represents sincerity without pretence, where acts of kindness come from the heart. Embedded in the spirit of Japanese culture, *omotenashi* is about anticipating the needs of others and creating an experience of warmth and authentic connection. True hospitality is not just about service but about honest care. How can you show up with care and intention in the spaces you create for others?

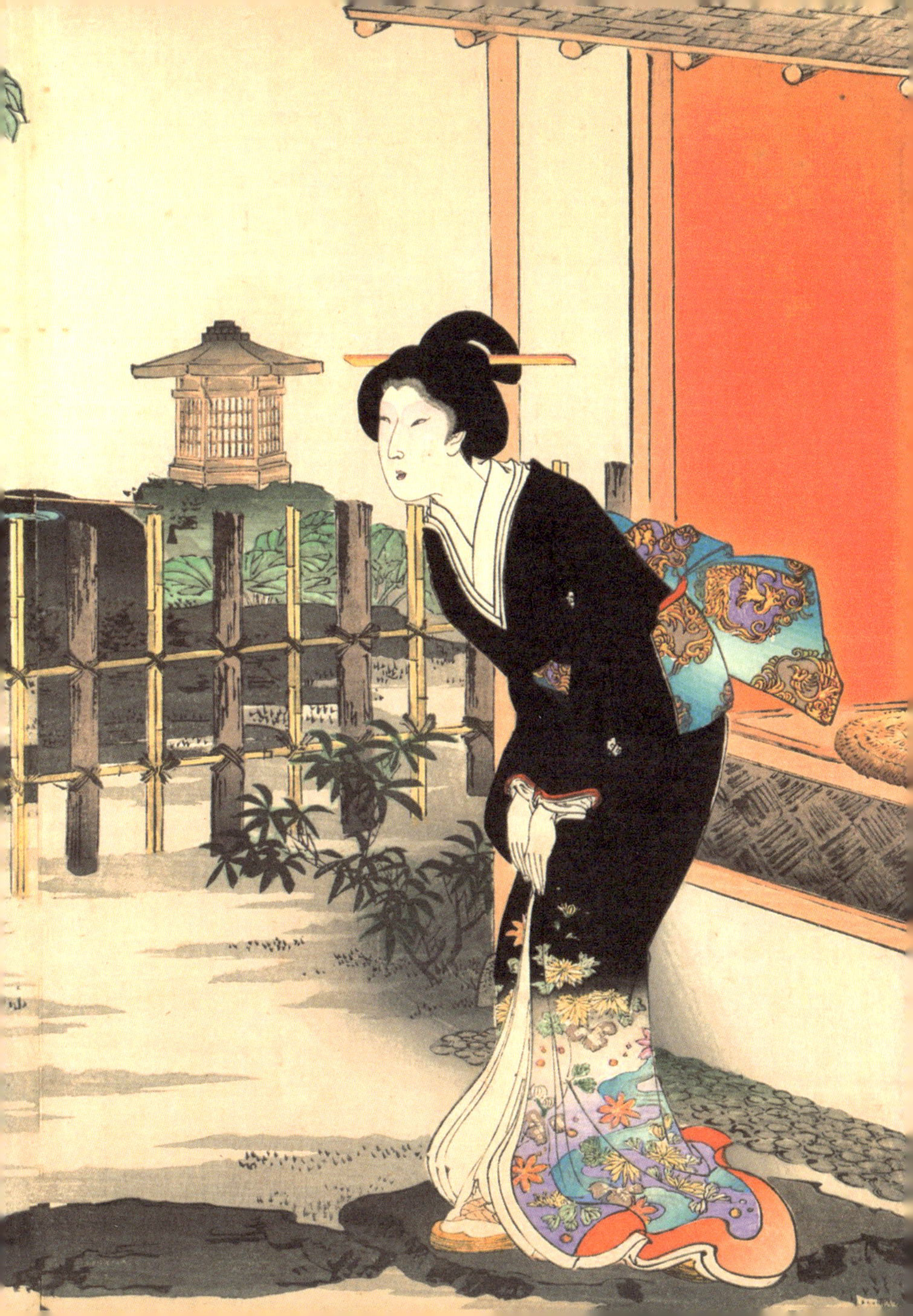

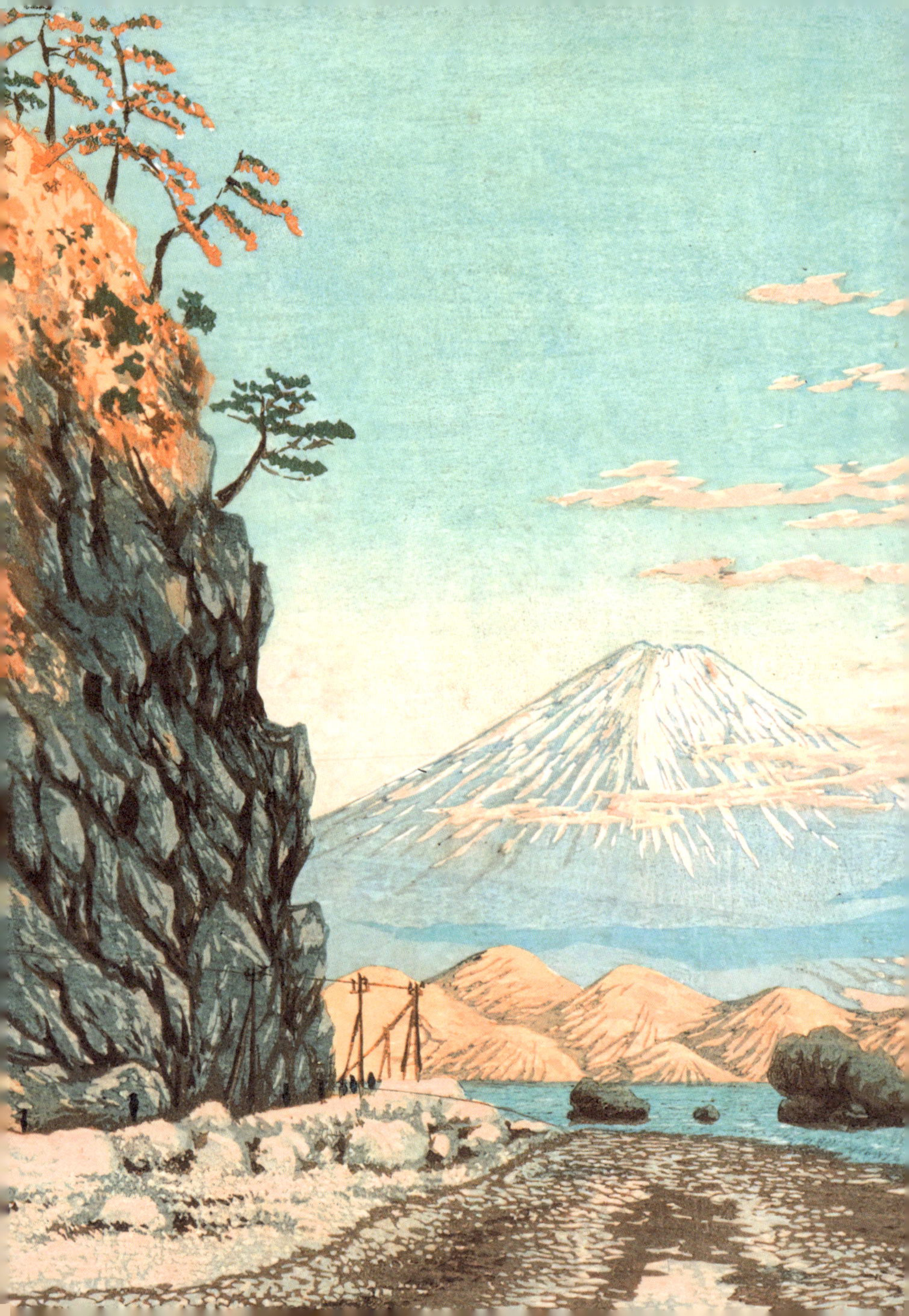

Daijōbu

大丈夫

Remember that it will be OK

One of Japan's most commonly used phrases, *daijōbu*, means 'it's OK' or 'it's alright'. Simple yet powerful, it embodies quiet strength and resilience, offering comfort in times of uncertainty. This phrase encourages us to find belief within ourselves, facing life's challenges with a calm and steady heart. It equally creates opportunities to connect with others, serving as a way to check in and provide reassurance. Let *daijōbu* give you solace, reminding you to trust in life's natural ebb and flow, embracing its ups and downs with grace and confidence.

EVERYDAY WISDOM

Hara hachi bun me

腹八分目

Nourish with moderation – leave space for ease

Hara hachi bun me, meaning 'eat until you are eighty per cent full', is a reminder of the wisdom in moderation. This saying invites us while eating to pause and listen to our body, recognizing that stopping before fullness nurtures health and longevity. Moderation is not deprivation but an act of balance that honours our well-being. Reflect on your choices at the table and in life: are they thoughtful, intentional and aligned with what you truly need? Let *hara hachi bun me* inspire you to cultivate harmony through mindful eating, creating space for both vitality and contentment.

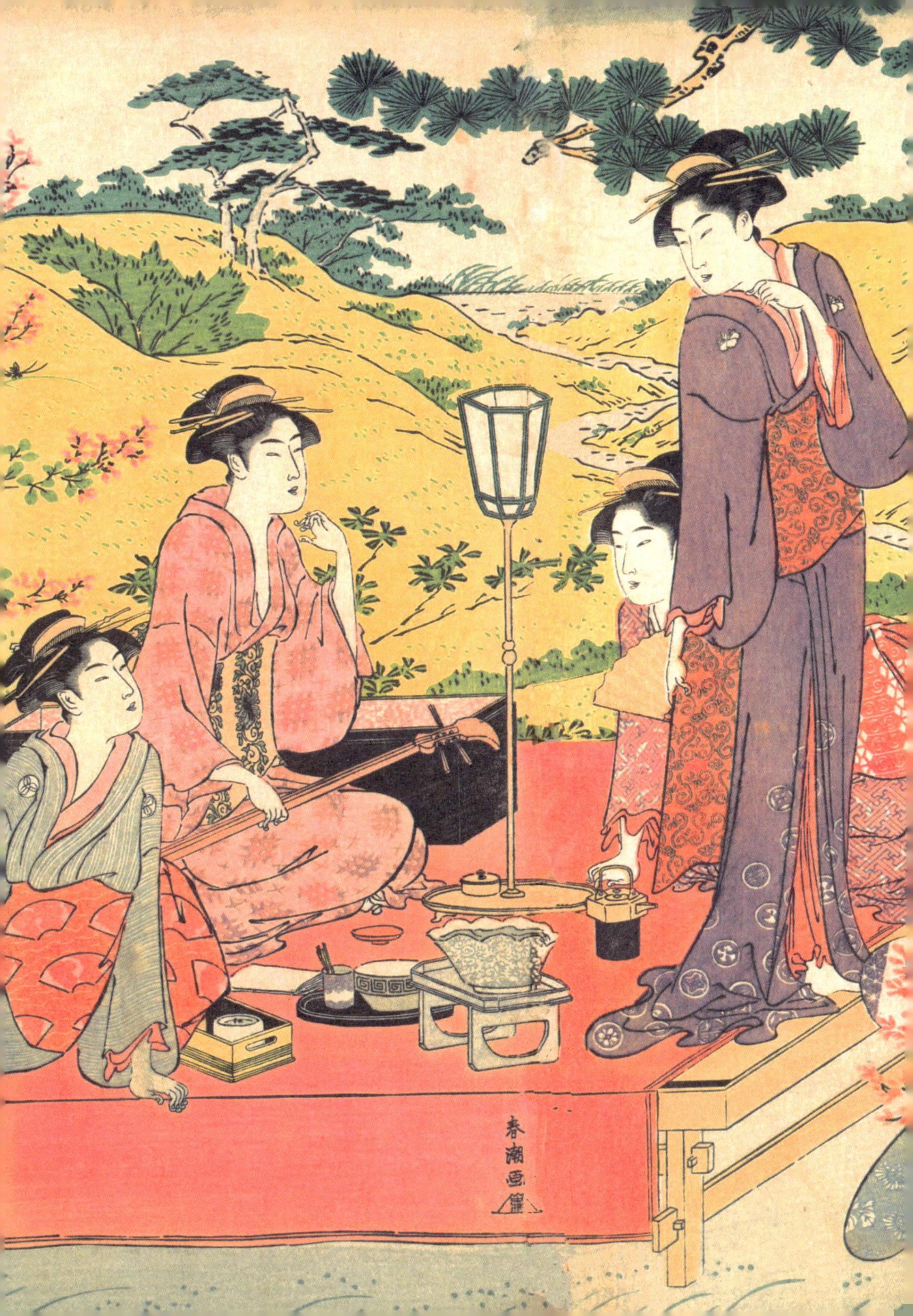
春潮画筆

たちあらふ岩製

きさのうらと
よひ日ことに
かくさくら

さゝなみや
ちゝの浦風
吹立て
うこくかしら
かさきの松
甲斐郡路
一菱郡路

天雲中よ
椎くよるゝと
きいて
とゝむ
志之庄氏や
長寿

Keizoku wa chikara nari

継続は力なり

Strength comes from consistency

Keizoku wa chikara nari teaches us that one's ability is built not through talent or performance alone but through steady, deliberate effort over time. This proverb encourages us to focus on showing up, even in small ways, rather than striving for perfection. Consistency is the foundation of greatness. By committing to regular practice, we cultivate quiet strength and endurance, empowering us to persevere through challenges and create meaningful, lasting impact.

Ma

間

Make room for the pause

Ma is the wisdom of the spaces in between. While we often feel the urge to fill every moment – with words, tasks or noise – *ma* teaches us the importance of allowing space to exist. These pauses offer clarity, the silence to reflect and the presence to fully experience life. Just as a pause in music makes the next note more powerful, *ma* reminds us that meaning often lies in these intermissions. How can you create space in your life to embrace the richness of the in-between? Notice the pauses in your day and intentionally create space for them. In these quiet moments, observe what feelings arise without needing to change them.

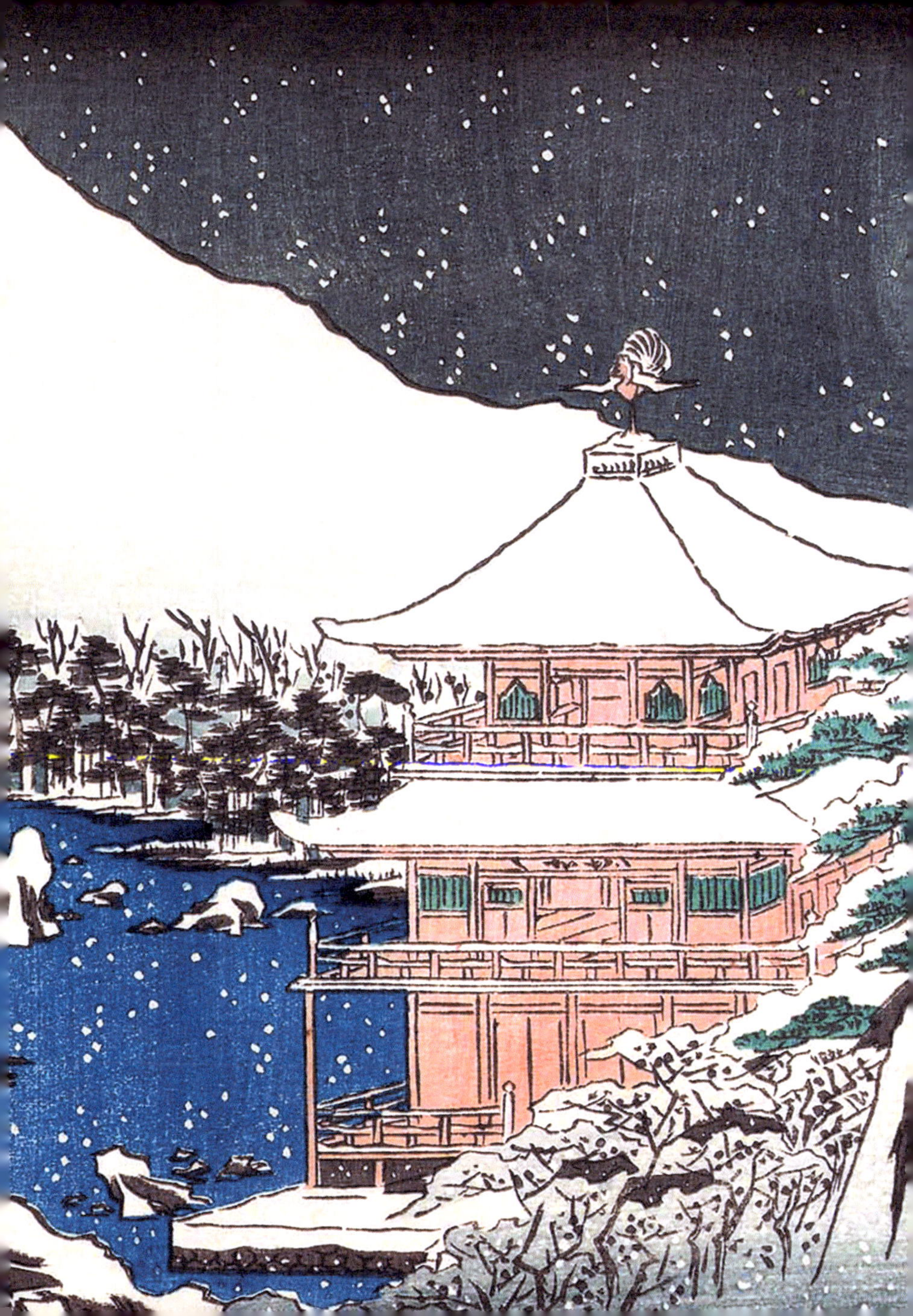

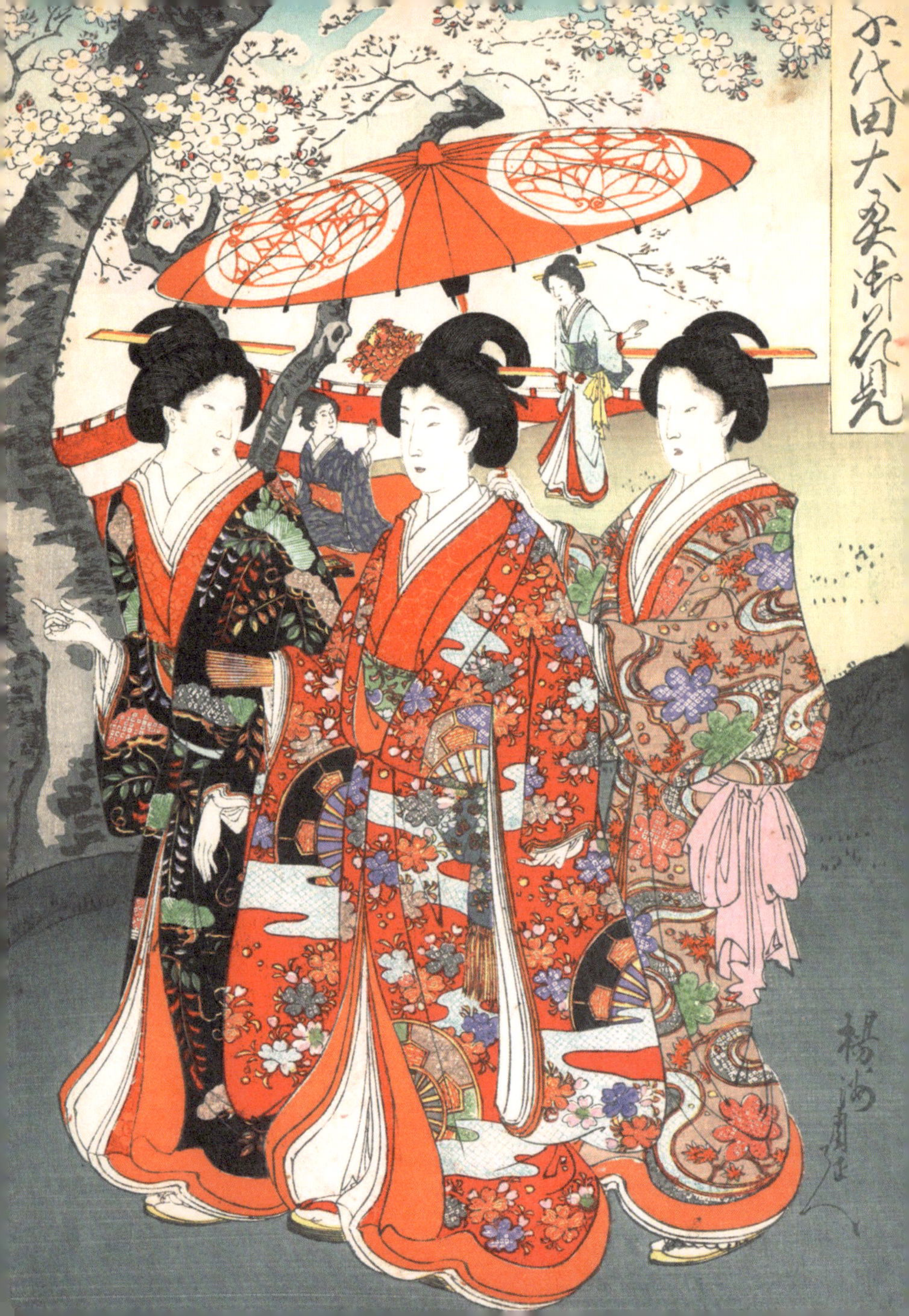
千代田大奥御花見
楊洲周延

Jūnin-toiro

十人十色

Celebrate diversity – the fabric of belonging

The Japanese proverb 'ten people, ten colours' highlights the beauty of diversity, celebrating the unique traits, perspectives and paths each person brings to life. It can be easy to fall into the comparison trap, measuring our worth against others, but *jūnin-toiro* helps us break free from this cycle, reminding us to appreciate the differences that make us distinct and authentic. By honouring this idiom, we foster mutual respect and authentic understanding for ourselves and those around us. Our diversity isn't only natural but essential for the vibrancy of the collective whole.

Shōganai

しょうがない

Let go to move forward

Shōganai embodies the wisdom of accepting what is beyond our control – not as passive surrender but as an active choice. It takes humility to recognize that some circumstances cannot be changed, and resisting them only drains our energy. By embracing *shōganai*, we cultivate resilience, agency and inner strength. Where in your life can you actively release resistance to what you cannot control? Choose to let go to create the needed space to move forward with clarity and purpose.

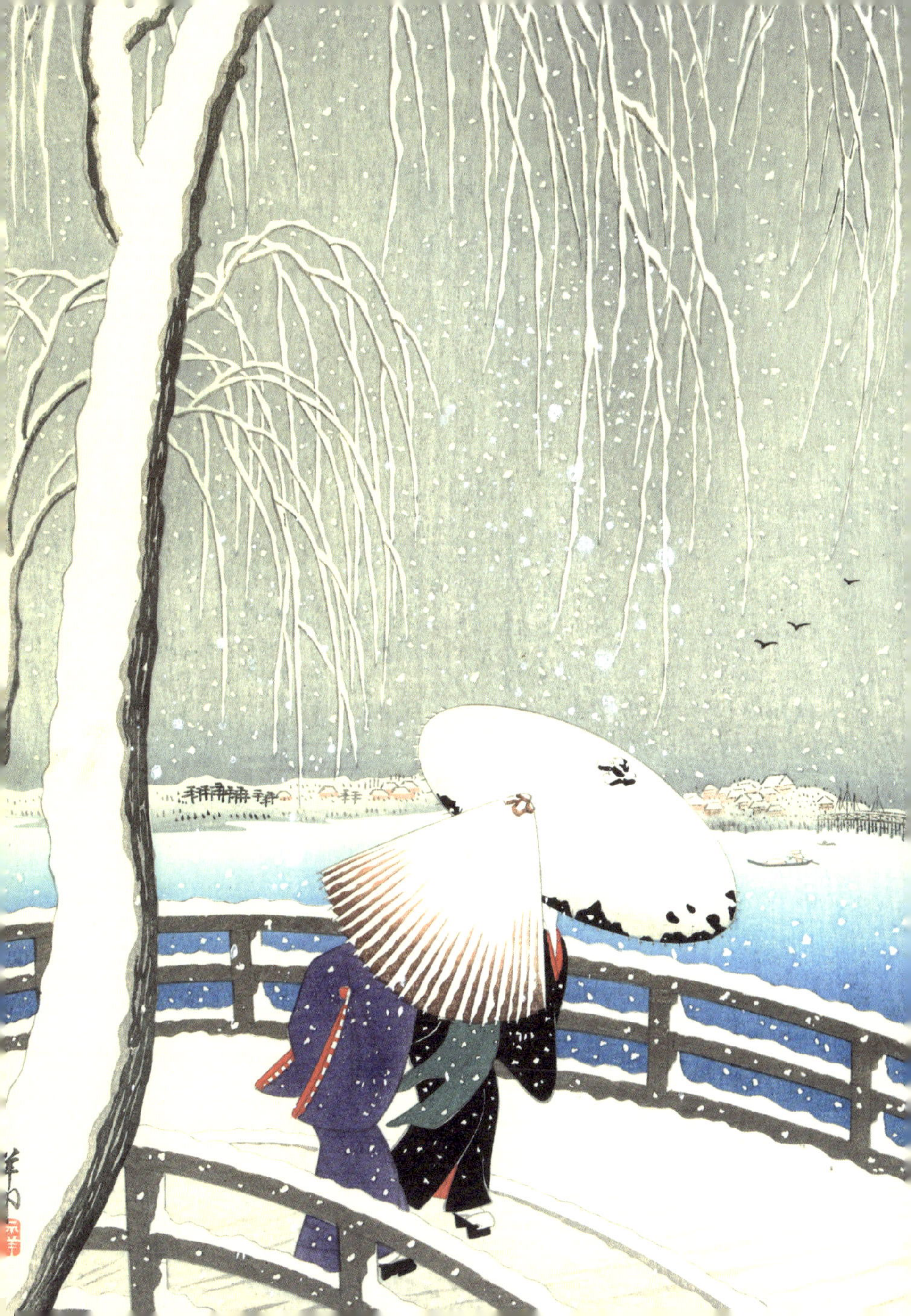

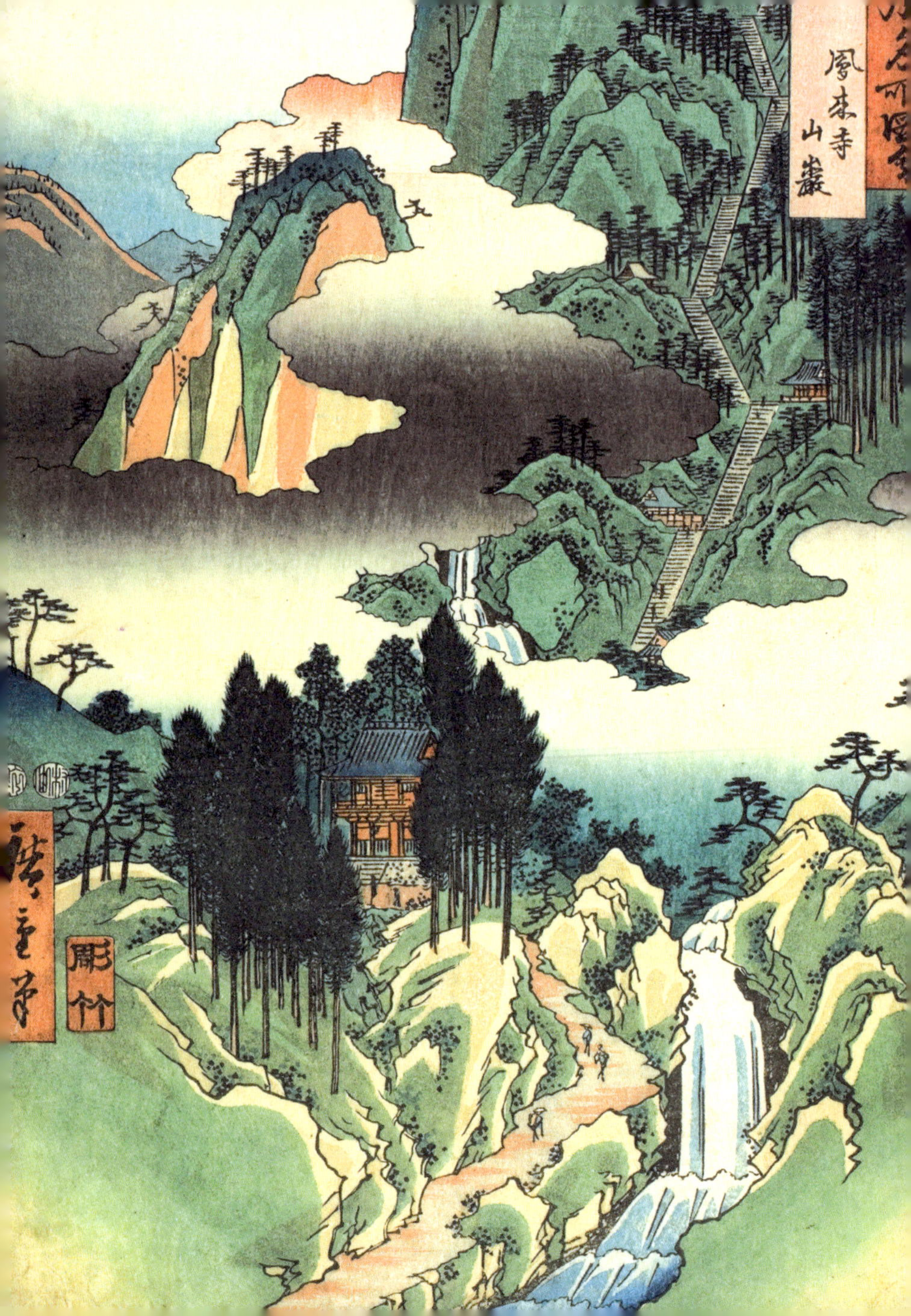
鳳来寺
山巌
廣重筆
彫竹

EVERYDAY WISDOM

Senri no michi mo ippo kara

千里の道も一歩から

A journey of a thousand miles begins with a single step

This Japanese proverb teaches that no matter how daunting or challenging a goal may seem, it always starts with a small, intentional action. It's natural to feel overwhelmed when facing a journey that appears too grand, ambitious or difficult. In these moments, focus solely on taking the first step, knowing that any forward movement is progress. Let this wisdom guide you to take deliberate action, reminding you that every step forward builds momentum to transform the most distant aspirations into reality.

Itadakimasu

いただきます

I will humbly receive this meal with gratitude

Before every meal, place your hands together in front of your chest, palms facing each other, and say '*itadakimasu*', meaning 'I humbly receive'. This everyday gesture is an act of mindfulness and gratitude, acknowledging the life that sustains us, the farmers who grew the food and the hands that prepared the meal. By pausing to say '*itadakimasu*', we honour the interconnectedness of life and approach each meal with humility and appreciation. Take the time to be present and grateful at each meal through *itadakimasu* and reflect on the energy and effort that nourishes our body and soul.

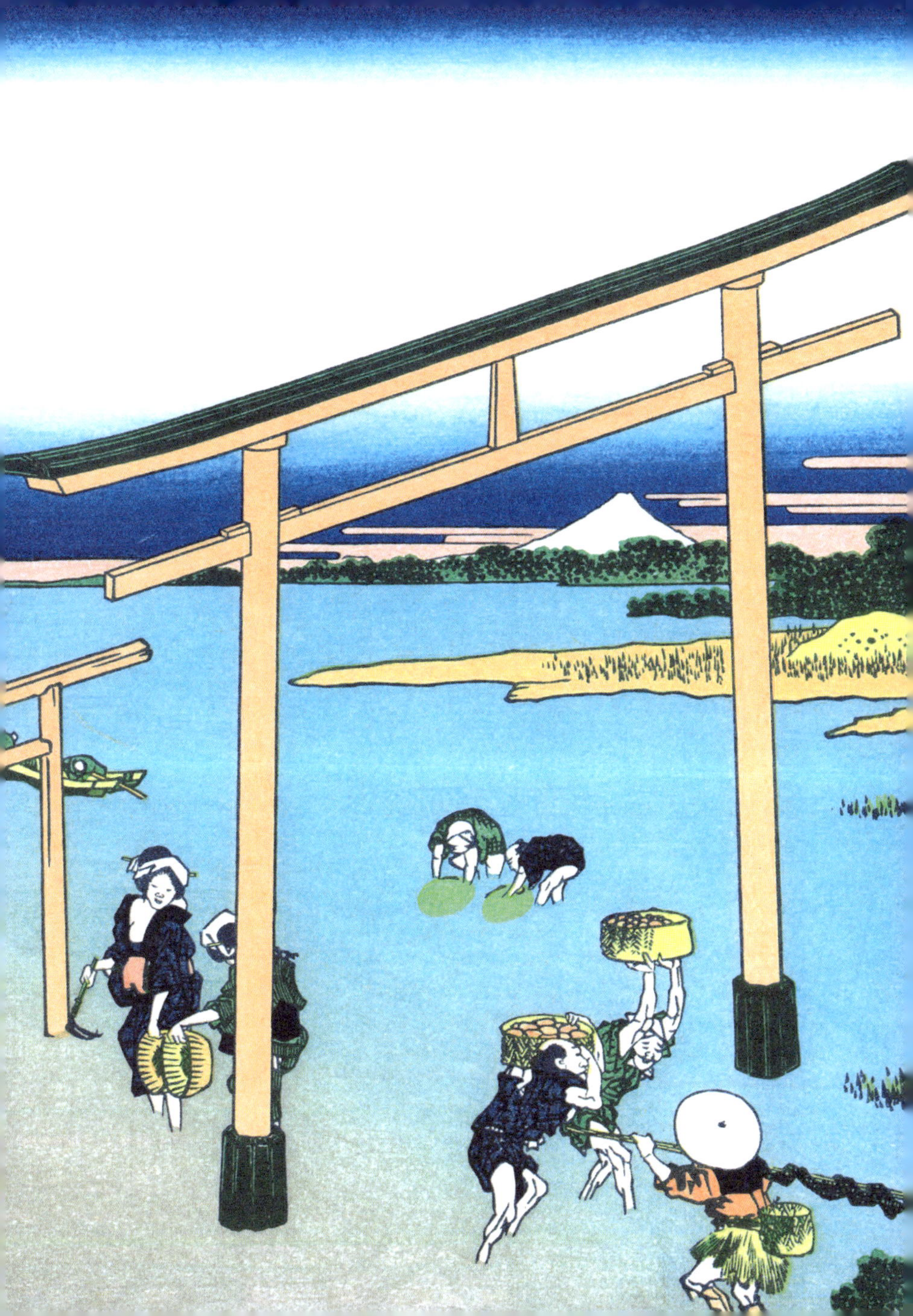

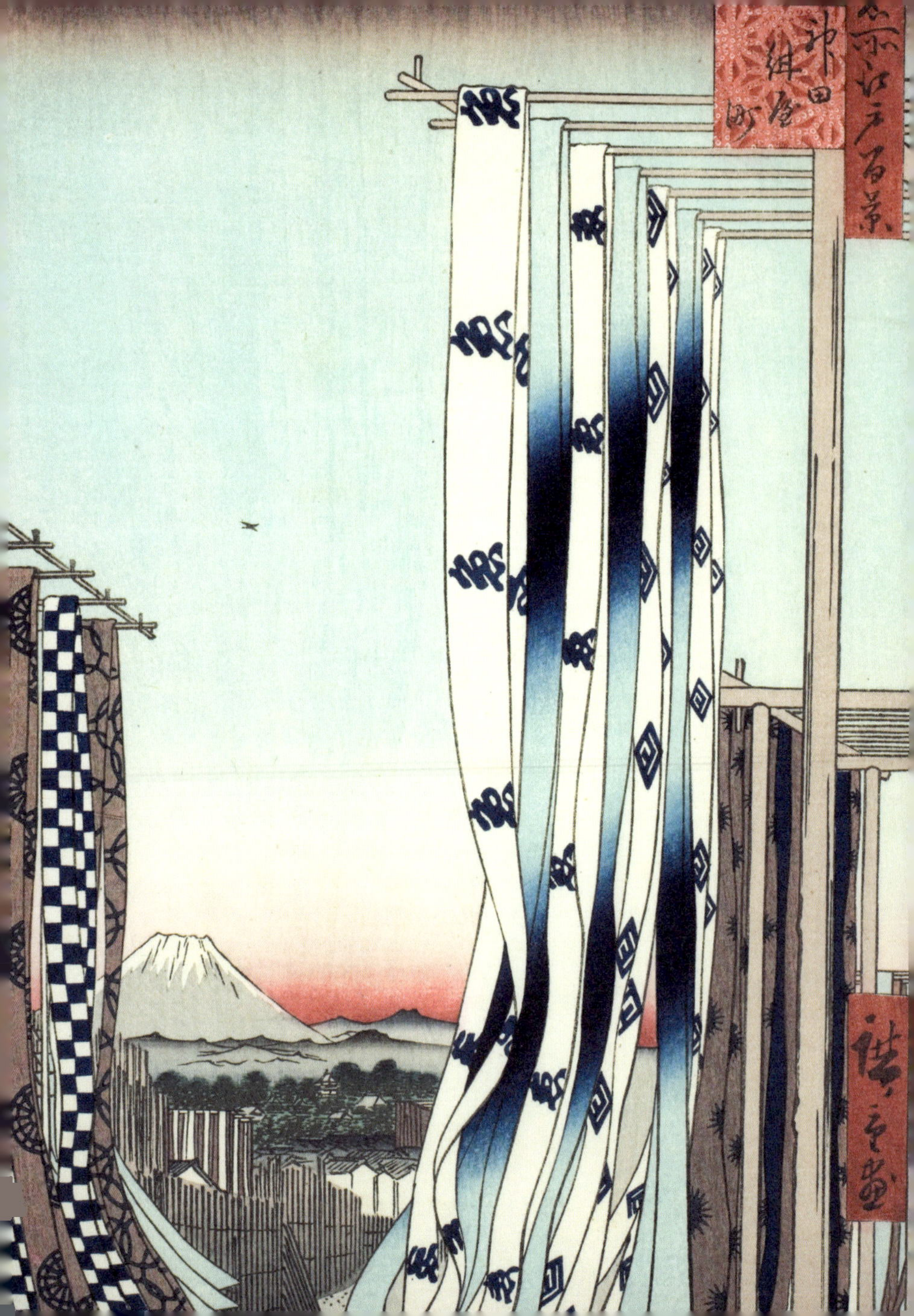
江戸百景
神田紺屋町

EVERYDAY WISDOM

Mottainai

もったいない

Honour the value in all things

Mottainai is the wisdom of recognizing and respecting the value in everything, from resources and time to opportunities or even one's potential. Rooted in traditional Japanese values and Buddhist teachings, it urges us to live with mindfulness, avoid waste and cherish what we have. More than just sustainability, *mottainai* is a way of seeing the world. Let us honour what we have, nurture our potential and cultivate respect for ourselves, our community and our environment. Before throwing something away, ask yourself: could this still serve a purpose? This week, try repurposing or donating just one item and reflect on what you already have. By embracing *mottainai*, we move through life with greater awareness and appreciation, ensuring that nothing is taken for granted.

Nana korobi ya oki

七転び八起き

Fall seven times, rise eight

This Japanese proverb embodies the wisdom of resilience and perseverance. Rise after every fall, knowing that resilience is not in avoiding challenges but learning and growing from them. Life's journey will inevitably have challenges, yet each setback is an opportunity to adapt and move forward. We are not measured by how many times we fail but by our ability to keep trying. Let this proverb remind you that no matter how many times you fall, you have the strength to rise again with courage and unwavering determination.

冨嶽三十六景 神奈川沖浪裏

婦人風俗尽
雙六

Yutori

ゆとり

Live with spaciousness

Do you have room in your life – mentally, physically and spiritually – to breathe, reflect and grow? Balance is more than time management; it's about creating space to nurture your well-being and reconnect with what truly matters. Slow down and embrace unhurried, intentional living that opens the space for life to unfold. Let *yutori* remind you that spaciousness is neither laziness nor indulgence – it is essential for living with greater ease, purpose and authenticity.

Isogaba maware

急がば回れ

Rushing will have you going in circles

Haste often leads to repeated mistakes, unexpected setbacks and wasted time. Though a slower, more measured approach may feel inefficient at first, it is often the smoothest path to success. When we recognize that rushing creates more obstacles than progress, we can learn to embrace the wisdom of moving with intention. Slowing down does not mean stagnation – it is a strategy for lasting success. What areas of your life could benefit from a more deliberate pace, bringing greater clarity and purpose?

名所雨図会
山伏谷

歌舞伎百姿

盆の月

EVERYDAY WISDOM

Warau kado ni wa fuku kitaru

笑う門には福来る

Laughter invites good fortune

Joy is not simply an expression of life but a force that shapes it. Just as this proverb suggests that fortune comes to those with laughter, remember that a light-hearted spirit attracts vibrant and warm energy, uplifting not only yourself but your environment and community. Even in challenging moments, choosing to find a silver lining can shift our perspective and create space for joy to grow. How can you bring more laughter into your life and open the door for the good waiting to enter?

Chiri mo tsumoreba yama to naru

塵も積もれば山となる

Small, repeated actions can create meaningful change

Like 'dust accumulating to form a mountain', this proverb reminds us that even the smallest efforts can build something remarkable when repeated over time. We often underestimate the quiet power of consistency and overestimate the need for grand gestures. Yet, meaningful progress is built on steady, intentional steps. What small action can you take today, knowing it will shape something greater over time? Trust in the quiet momentum of persistence – it is how mountains of progress are made.

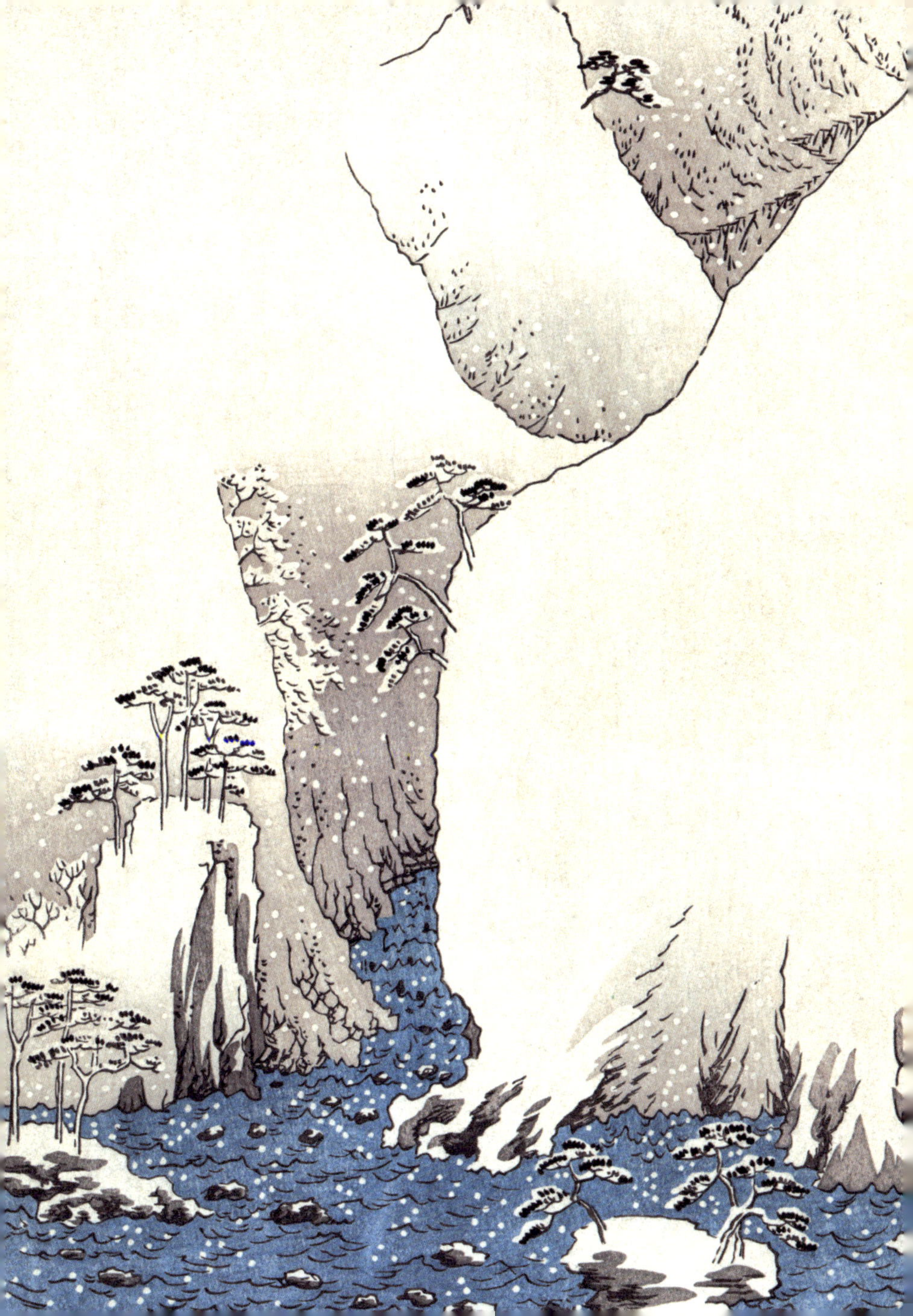

紀伊 和歌三浦

INNER WORLD

Kū

空

Create space like the open sky in your everyday

Often translated as 'emptiness', *kū* is not the absence of something but the presence of possibility. With the character's additional meaning of 'sky', it represents vast openness, free from limitation. Like an overfilled glass, taking on too much leaves no room for anything new to enter. Reflect on what you are carrying – can you release something to create space for transformation? Embrace the wisdom of *kū*, trusting that intentional space invites new beginnings and fresh opportunities into your life.

INNER WORLD

Ikigai

生き甲斐

Embrace the everyday moments that make life worth living

Ikigai is your reason for being – the quiet force that brings joy, meaning and purpose to your days. It isn't defined by profession, achievement or external validation but begins with an inner knowing and holistic understanding of what makes life fulfilling. A key contributor to longevity, *ikigai* is found in the simple and joyful moments that sustain us – whether through connection, purpose or acts of care. What brings you energy? Reflect on what nourishes your soul and fuels you every day, and take action to align your life with what matters.

名所江戸百景
浅草田甫

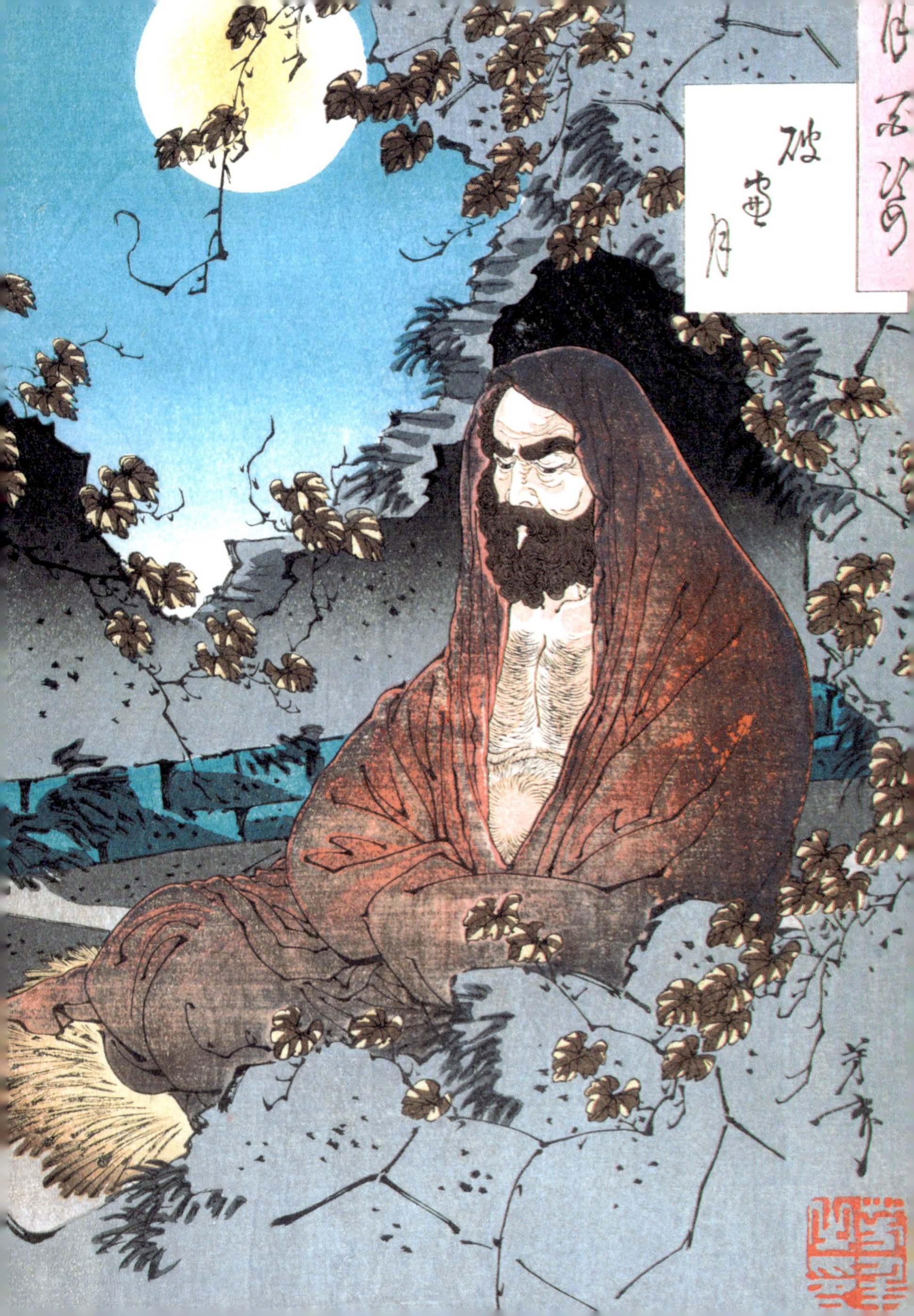
破窓月

Mushō-shin

無生心

Cultivate an unburdened, free heart

Mushō-shin is a Zen principle describing a state where the heart and mind exist in absolute freedom. While its characters can suggest an 'empty heart', this is not a void but rather a state of profound truth where the self is unshaped by judgment, attachment or distraction. Zen does not ask us to understand this intellectually but to experience it through deeply intentional meditation. In *mushō-shin*, layers of conditioning fall away, leaving only the pure essence of being – fully present, weightless and at ease. Set aside five minutes to sit quietly. Let go of judgment or expectation. Simply observe your breath, your thoughts and the space between them – without holding on.

Mujū-shin

無住心

Exist beyond the self

Mujū-shin is a Zen principle that transcends the individual, dissolving the boundaries of the self to merge with the boundless flow of existence. More than detachment, it is a deep, experienced and felt state of interconnectedness where one's spirit is not fixed but moves freely, everywhere and anywhere. Expanding beyond *mushō-shin* and cultivated through dedicated meditation, *mujū-shin* is knowing that our existence is not confined to the self but part of a vast, limitless whole. In letting go of the self, we awaken to the truth that we are not separate – we are everything.

月耕随筆

龍昇天

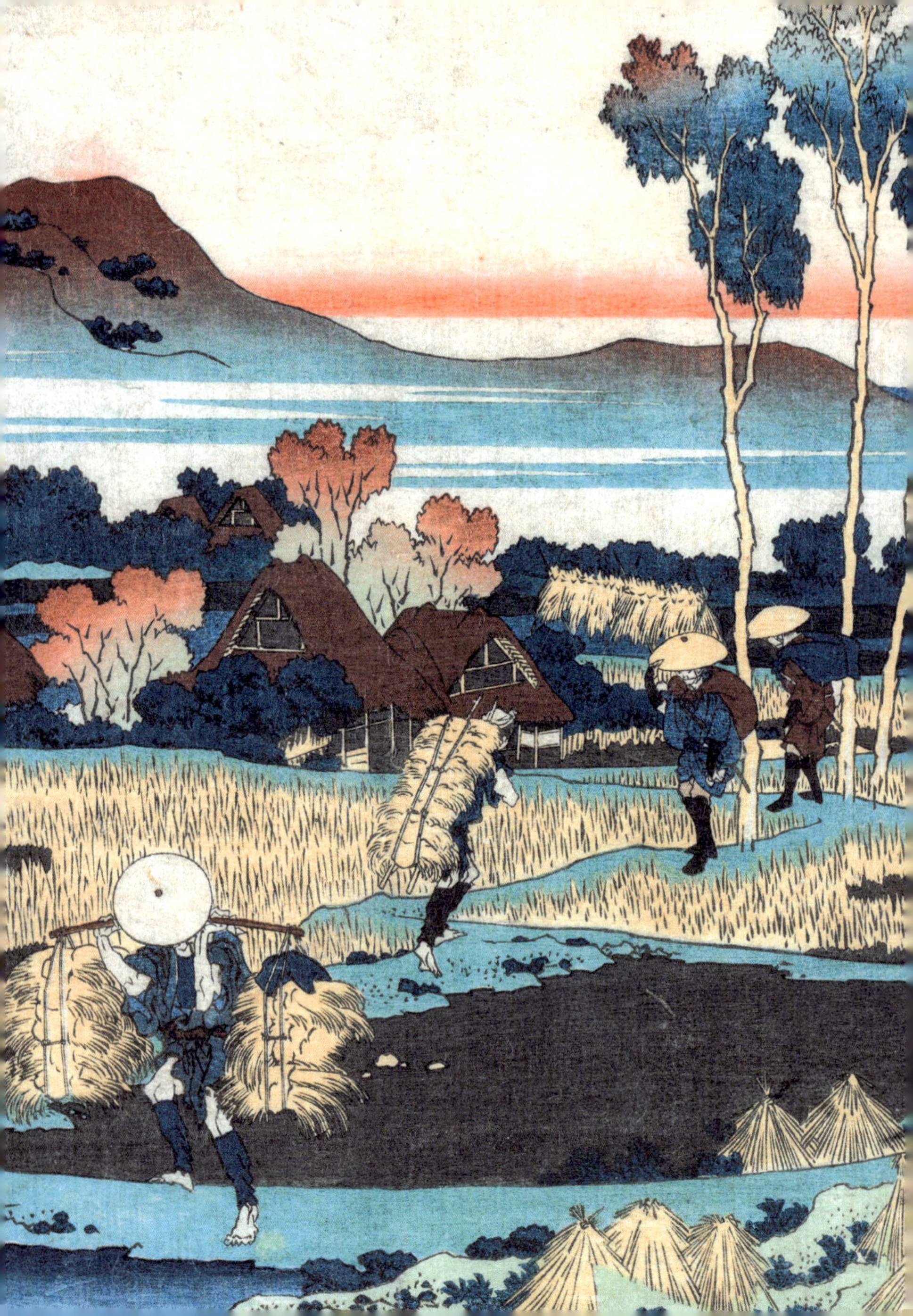

INNER WORLD

Jitōmyō

自灯明

Be your own light

While our community can empower us, it is also just as important to remember to cultivate your own inner strength. *Jitōmyō*, which combines 自 (*ji*, one's 'self') and 灯明 (*tōmyō*, referring to a 'light'), encourages us to cultivate this inner strength and trust our own judgement. Remember that having your own back is essential, allowing us to find our inner light to guide our way forward.

Tamashī

魂

Connect with the spirit that fuels your life

Tamashī is the vital force that breathes energy into all living beings – humans, plants and animals alike. Traditionally seen as eternal, it exists beyond the physical body, connecting us to the greater flow of existence. Honouring *tamashī* means recognizing the unseen yet deeply felt energy that sustains both body and soul. When we embrace this vital spirit we recognize the beauty of our existence and our interconnectedness with all things. Close your eyes and connect with your *tamashī*. How can you honour your spirit today?

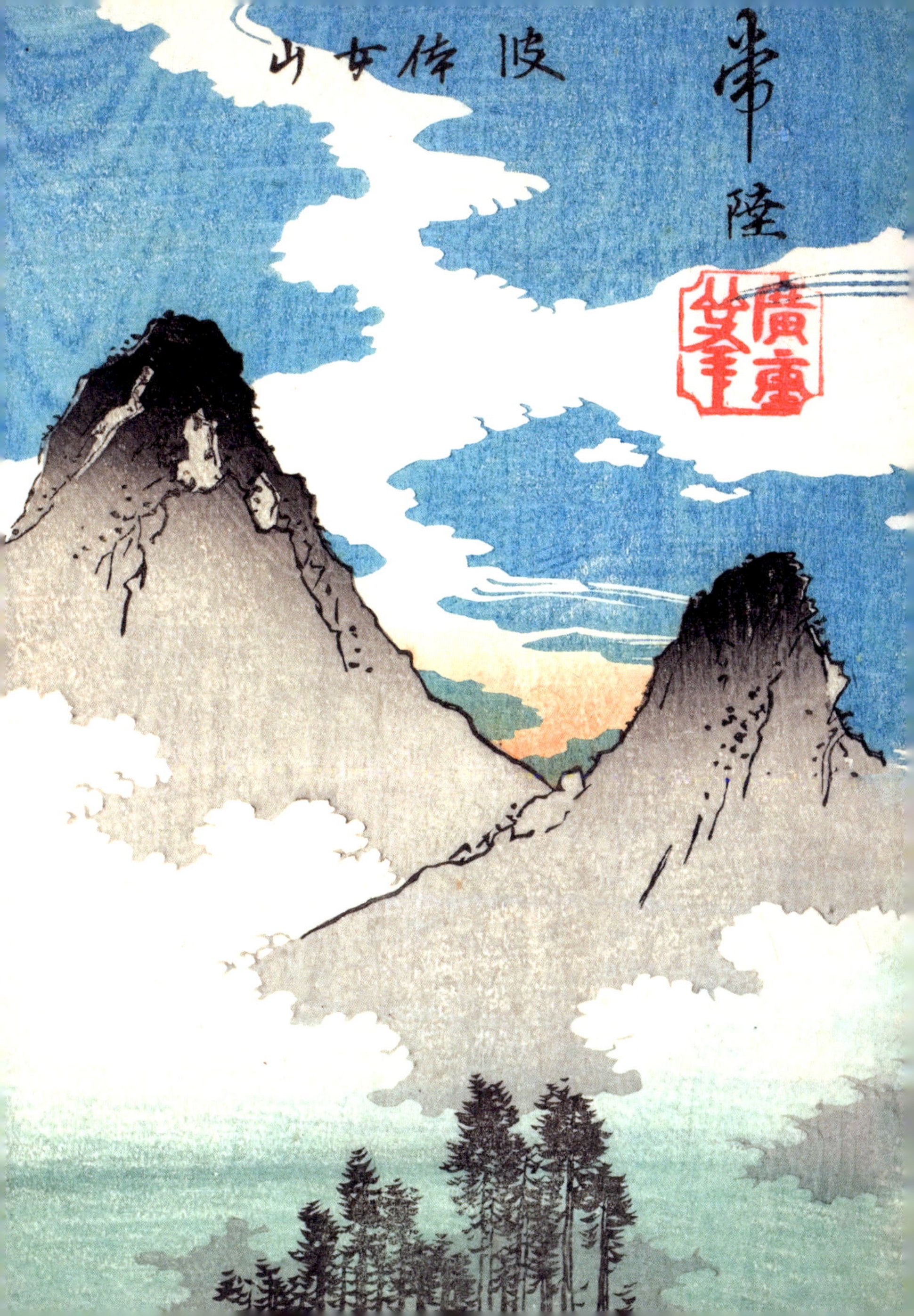
常陸
廣重筆

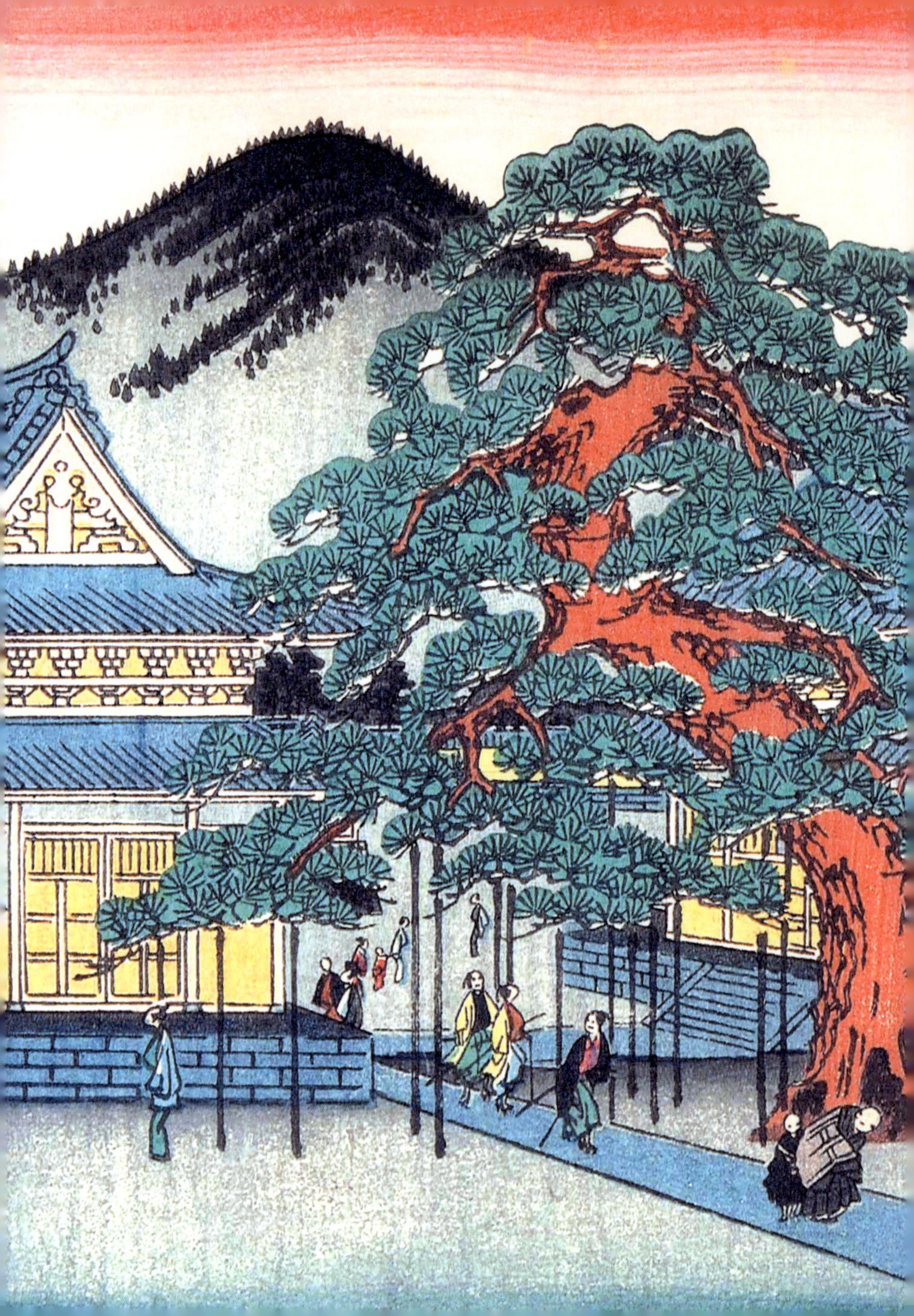

INNER WORLD

Zen

禅

Build an unburdened heart through meditation

Zen, originally a Japanese sect of Buddhism, extends far beyond the temple walls, shaping Japanese arts, architecture, martial arts, language and daily life. At its core, *zen* is the practice of looking inward – cultivating deep awareness through meditation to understand one's authentic self. While modern English often equates *zen* with a state of calm, its essence lies in the dedicated art of meditation. *Zen* is not just a state of mind but a practice – an ongoing effort to strip away distraction and illusion, revealing the freedom and presence that already exists within each of us. Choose one daily activity – such as washing dishes or cooking – and do it with full attention and no distractions. Let each movement, sensation and breath become a practice of presence.

INNER WORLD

Seijaku

静寂

Let silence guide you to serenity

Seijaku connects the many dimensions that arise in silence – from the lack of sound to a state of inner calm and mental tranquillity. It is the serenity found not in emptiness but in quiet strength. When the world feels loud, *seijaku* reminds us to choose stillness. Slow down, observe with intention, and reconnect with your inner centre. Create space in your day to embrace the absence of noise so you can begin to hear the quiet wisdom of your soul. Find a quiet moment in your day, free from screens or noise, and gently check in with yourself: how are you really feeling? Listen without trying to fix.

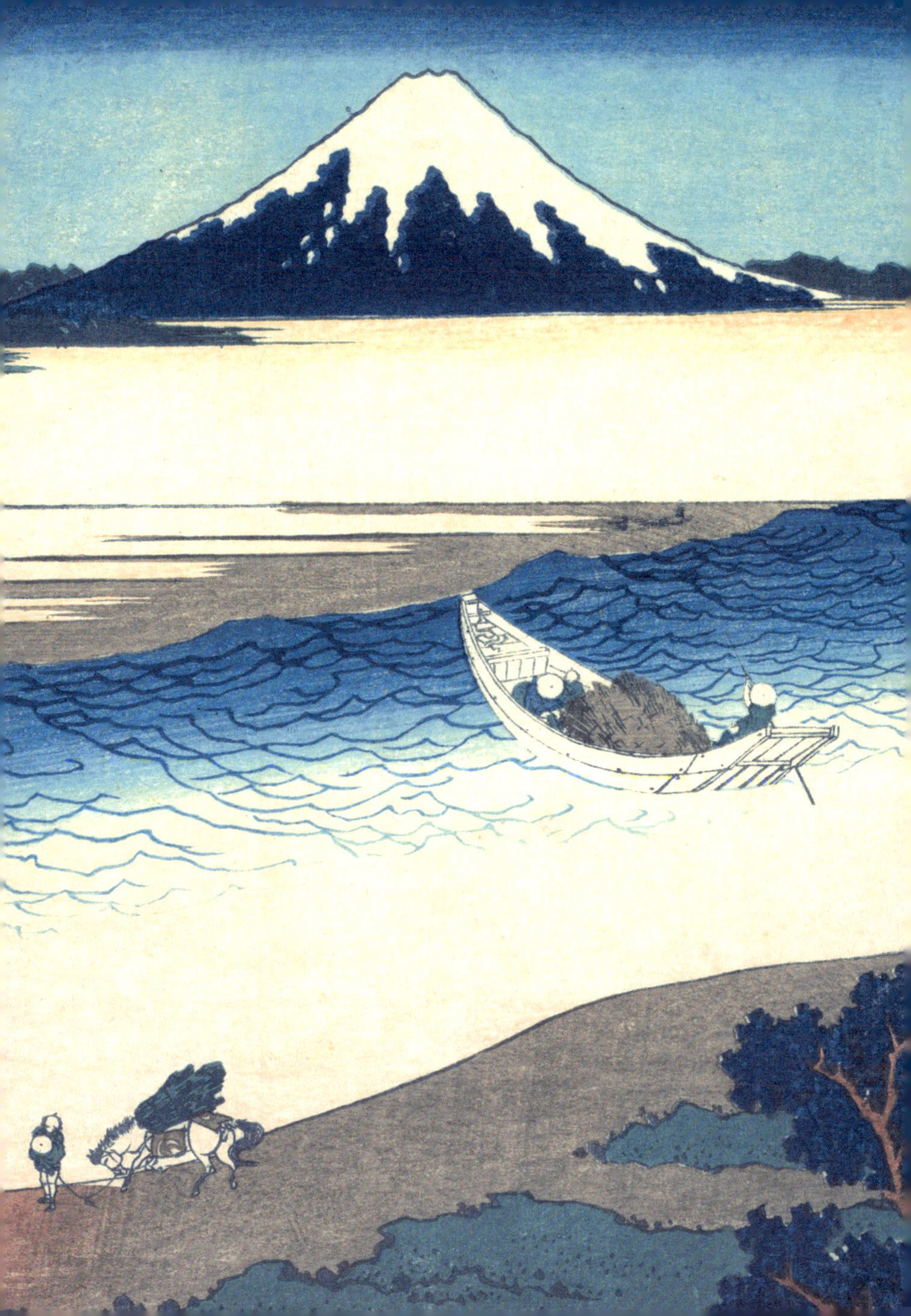

五十三次名所圖會
十三
沼津
足柄山不二嵜
廣重

Kokorozashi

志

Where is your heart longing to go?

Kokorozashi, the Japanese word for 'intention', embodies the wisdom of aligning with the direction your heart desires to follow. The character 志 combines 心 (*kokoro*, meaning 'heart and soul') with 士 (*shi*, derived from 之, symbolizing 'footprints marking the first step'). True intention is more than desire — it's a commitment to take action. Reflect on your heart's aspirations and take purposeful steps towards them. Lead with your heart to transform your dreams into meaningful progress, creating a life rooted in authenticity and purpose.

Seijitsu

誠実

Embody sincerity through word and action

Seijitsu captures the beauty of living truthfully, where words and actions align with integrity. The characters 誠 (*makoto*, 'a heart without falsehood') and 実 (*jitsu*, 'substance') emphasize that sincerity must be lived wholeheartedly, beyond mere intention. Genuine sincerity is felt when our values shine consistently through speech and action, building trust and authenticity. Reflect on a recent moment when your words and actions were aligned – or not. What would it look like today to move through the day with sincerity? Let *seijitsu* guide you to cultivate this alignment within yourself and surround yourself with others with the same depth of honesty and integrity.

士五十七區　矢頭右衛七　近習長助之男二十石五人扶持　行年十八

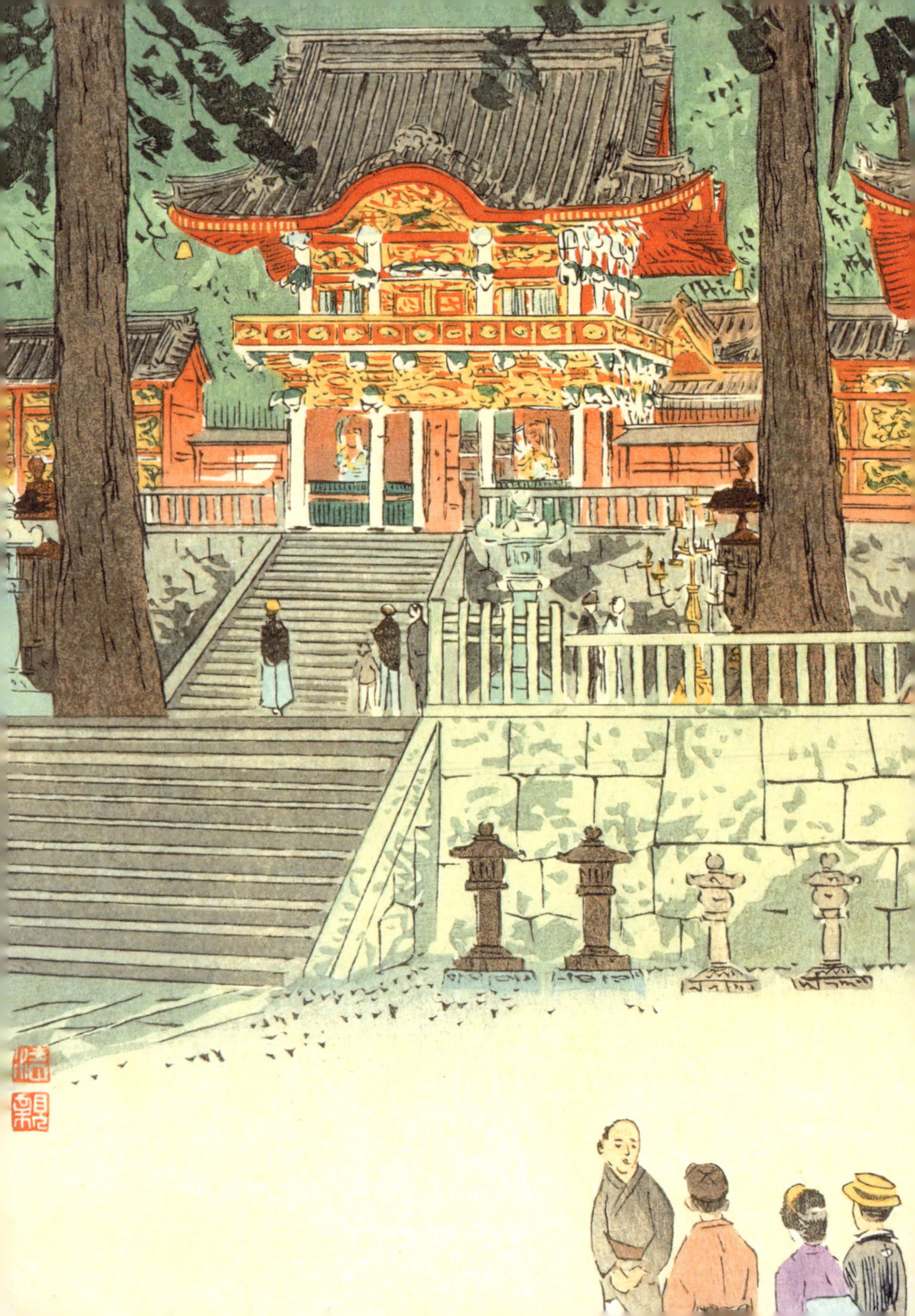

INNER WORLD

Tenmei

天命

Walk in your destined path

Tenmei represents destiny – one's higher calling, the path uniquely laid out by fate. But fate is not passive; it is a guiding force that calls us to recognize and walk in our purpose with clarity and courage. In a world of distractions, it is easy to drift away from what truly matters. Reflect on the direction of your life: are you walking the path that aligns with your true calling? Trust in the wisdom of *tenmei*, honouring the journey that is uniquely yours with faith and courage.

Kaika

開花

Recognize the beauty of your becoming

Kaika, meaning 'blossoming', symbolizes the process of unfolding into your full potential. The characters 開 (*kai*, 'to open') and 花 (*ka*, 'flower') are a reminder that growth, like nature, cannot be rushed. Just as a flower blooms through patience and care, personal transformation happens when we nurture ourselves with intention. Trust in your own timing. Are you allowing yourself the space to grow? Honour the process, embrace the unfolding, and recognize that your journey – like a flower in bloom – is already a masterpiece in motion.

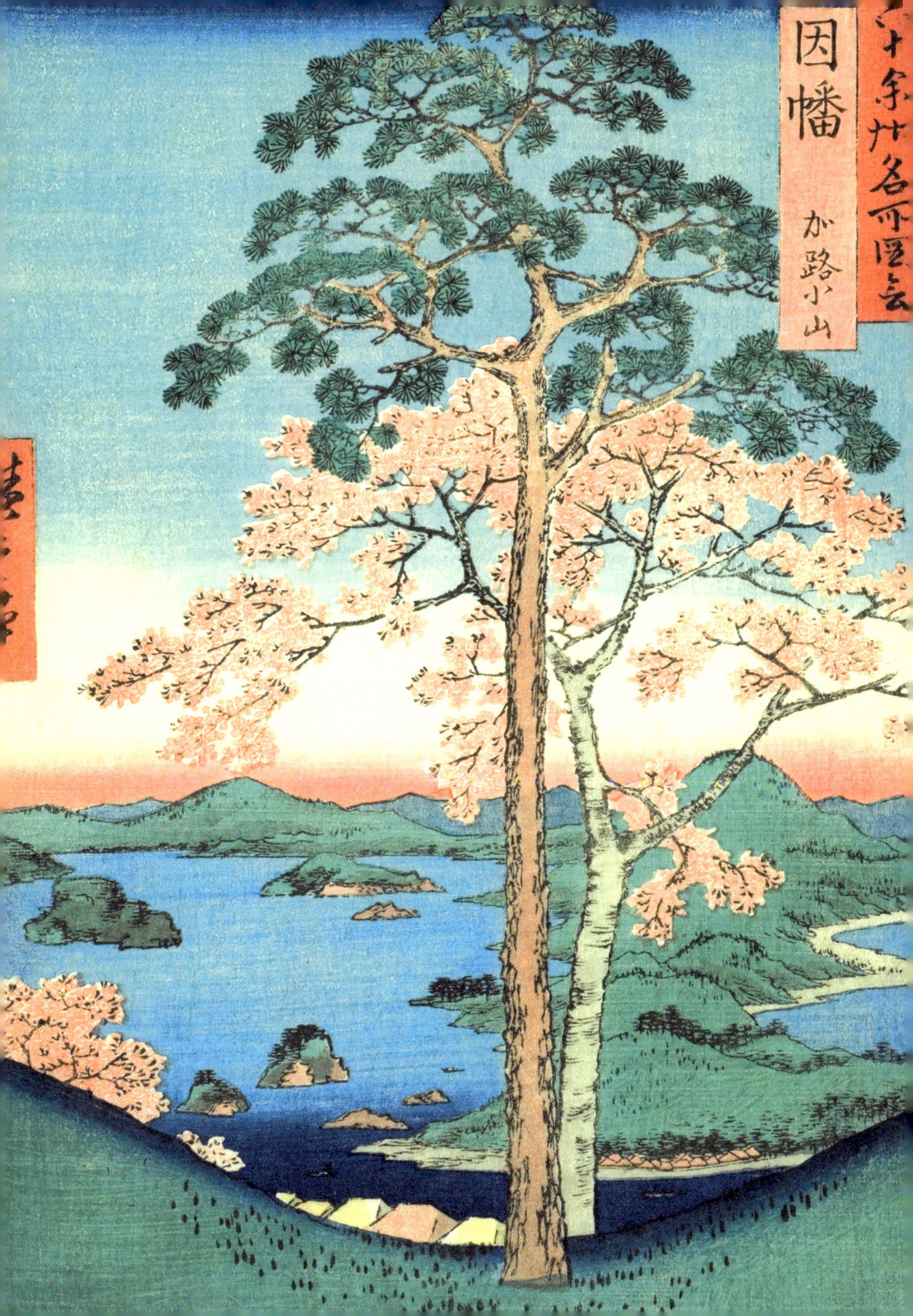
十余州名所図会
因幡
か路小山

名所江戸百景

堀切の花菖蒲

広重画

Setsunai

切ない

Cherish those moments when your heart tugs with bittersweetness

Setsunai is the ache of nostalgia, the pull of a past, transient moment that touches your heart. It represents the joy and sadness we feel when we cherish a memory, even as it gently slips away. *Setsunai* gives us the wisdom that impermanence is at the core of life's beauty, deepening our appreciation for what is fleeting but meaningful. Rather than resisting this ache, embrace it as proof of a deeply lived life. Reflect on what moments in your life hold the heart-tugging weight of *setsunai*. How do they shape the way you cherish what remains?

NATURE AND IMPERMANENCE

Kumo no ue wa itsumo hare

雲の上はいつも晴れ

Above the clouds, it's always sunny

This Japanese proverb reminds us that hope and positivity remain, even when hidden by life's challenges. When everything around us feels cloudy and uncertain, it's easy to feel discouraged. Yet, as the sun continues to shine beyond the clouds, brighter moments await even when we cannot see them. Let this wisdom reassure you in difficult times, encouraging patience and faith. Know that clarity and light will always return.

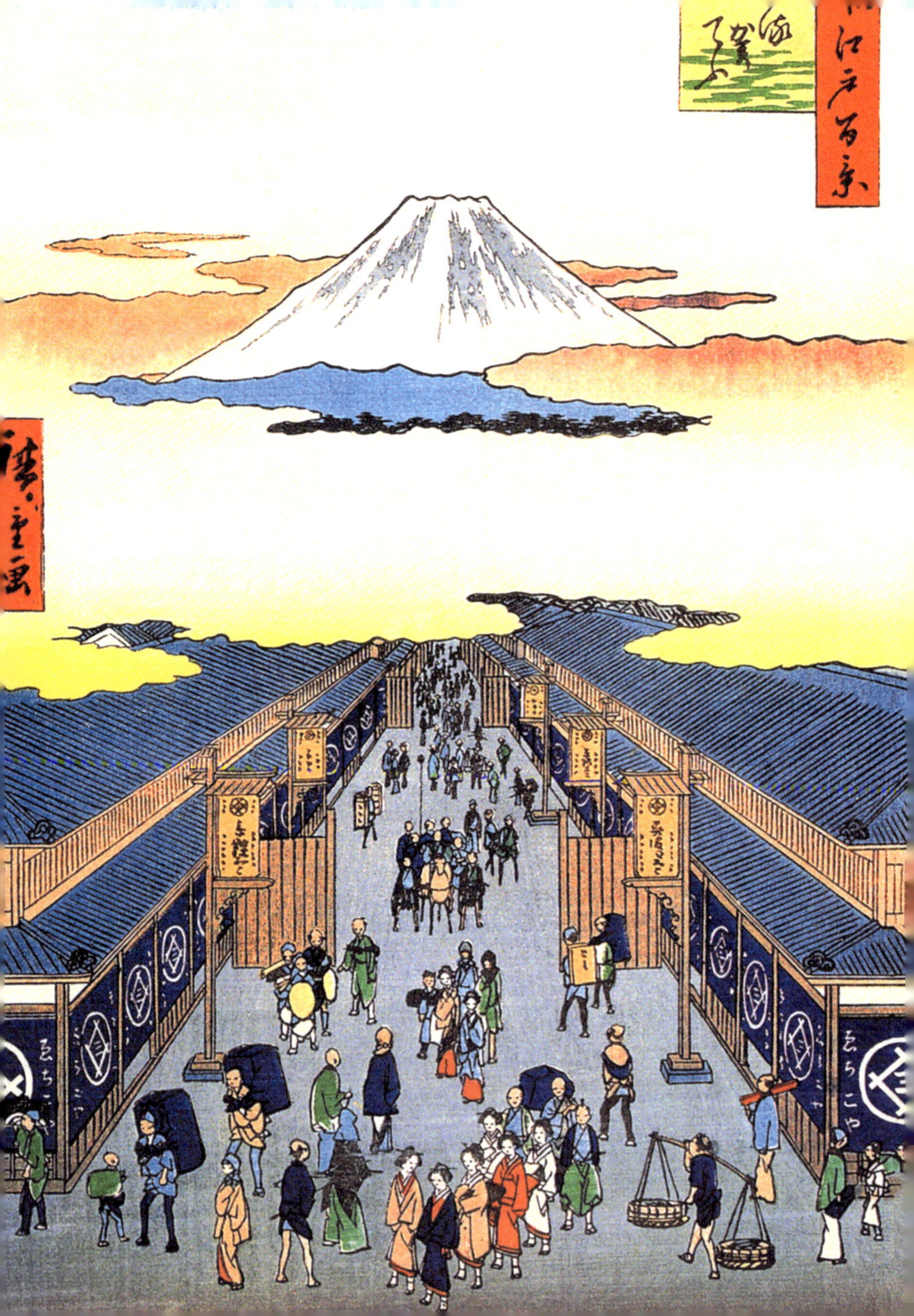
江戸百景
廣重画

嵐山

NATURE AND IMPERMANENCE

Ishi no ue ni mo sannen

石の上にも三年

Meaningful change takes time

The proverb 'three years on a rock' embodies the wisdom of patience and perseverance, reminding us that meaningful change takes time. Just as sitting on a cold rock for three years eventually warms it, steady commitment turns effort into progress. In a world that chases instant results, we often resist discomfort and doubt the power of slow change. However, true transformation requires discipline – the ability to keep going even when progress feels invisible. Trust in the quiet work of time. What are you willing to commit to, knowing that slow and consistent effort leads to lasting change? Choose one interest you want to nurture. Commit to it daily – even for five minutes – and gently track your consistency across the week.

Kōun ryūsui

行雲流水

Live like flowing clouds and running water

A core principle expressed in Japanese calligraphy, *kōun ryūsui* is a Japanese idiom that shares the wisdom of moving harmoniously with life's natural current. As a brush glides gracefully across paper, release resistance and embrace the flow. Beyond artistic expression, we can cultivate inner harmony and ease by accepting life's ever-changing rhythm. Try a free-flow journaling exercise. Let your hand move across the page without overthinking. Follow the current of your thoughts and emotions with curiosity and ease. Let *kōun ryūsui* remind you to let go, trusting and flowing gently with life's unfolding path.

春信画

六十余州名所図会
甲斐
猿橋
広重筆

NATURE AND IMPERMANENCE

Shinrin-yoku

森林浴

Spend time in nature to
reconnect with yourself

Often referenced internationally as 'forest bathing', *shinrin-yoku* is the practice of slowing down and mindfully connecting with the natural world through your five senses. Immerse yourself fully by noticing nature's beauty through touch, smell, hearing, sight and taste. Let it guide you out of your thoughts and into your body, restoring balance to your mind, body and soul. Nature is more than a backdrop – it is a gift. Engage with it wisely as a powerful source of healing, grounding and inner calm.

NATURE AND IMPERMANENCE

Komorebi

木漏れ日

Slow down and appreciate life's fleeting moments

Komorebi is the Japanese word for sunlight filtering through trees. It captures nature's quiet invitation to pause, breathe and appreciate serene, fleeting moments. Just as rays of light filter through the trees, creating a tranquil sense of peace, *komorebi* reminds us to notice and connect with the natural world. By embracing nature's ever-changing harmony of light and shadow, we learn to accept life's impermeance with grace. Let *komorebi* remind you to slow down and pay attention so you don't miss the beauty in these exquisite, passing moments.

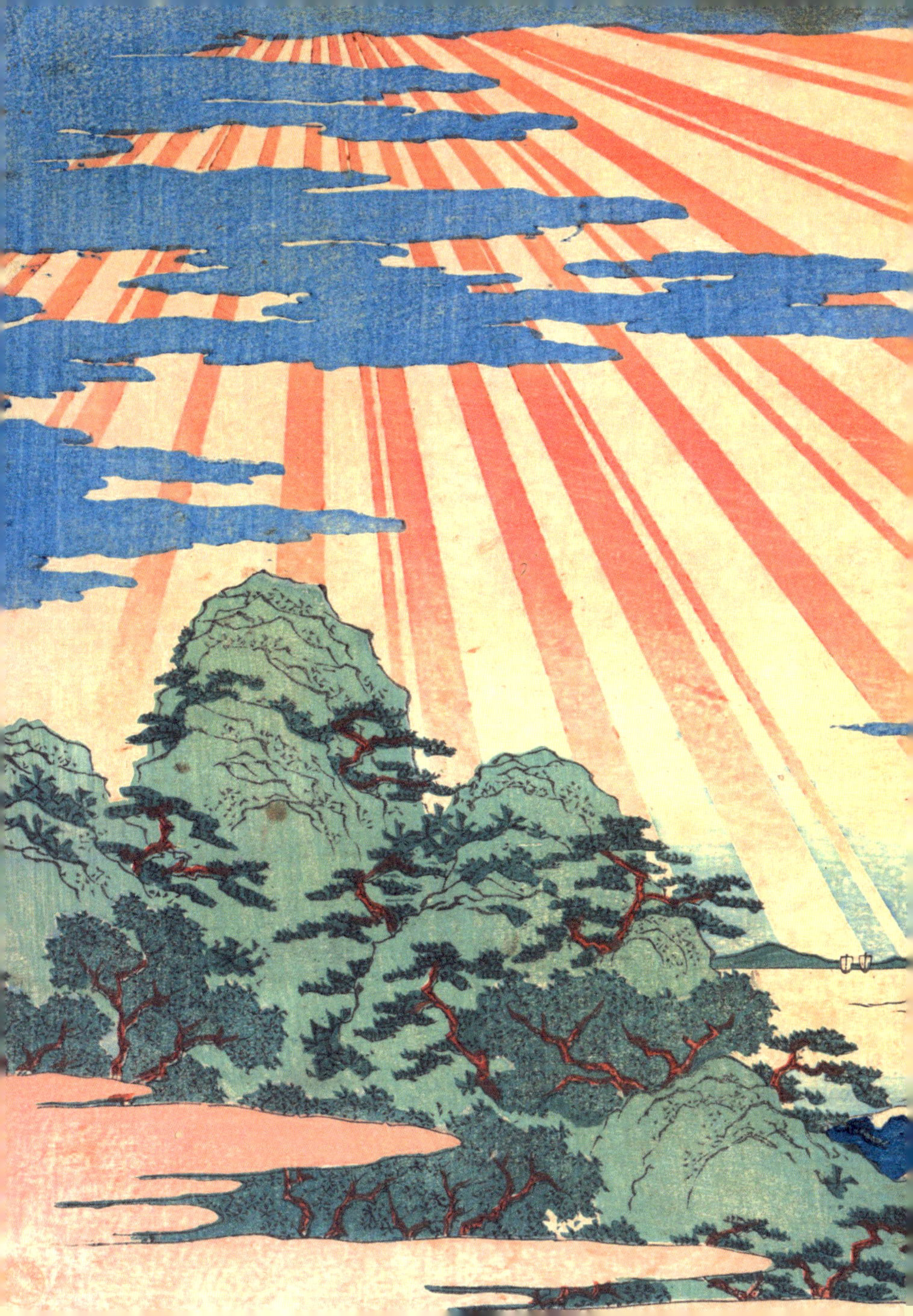

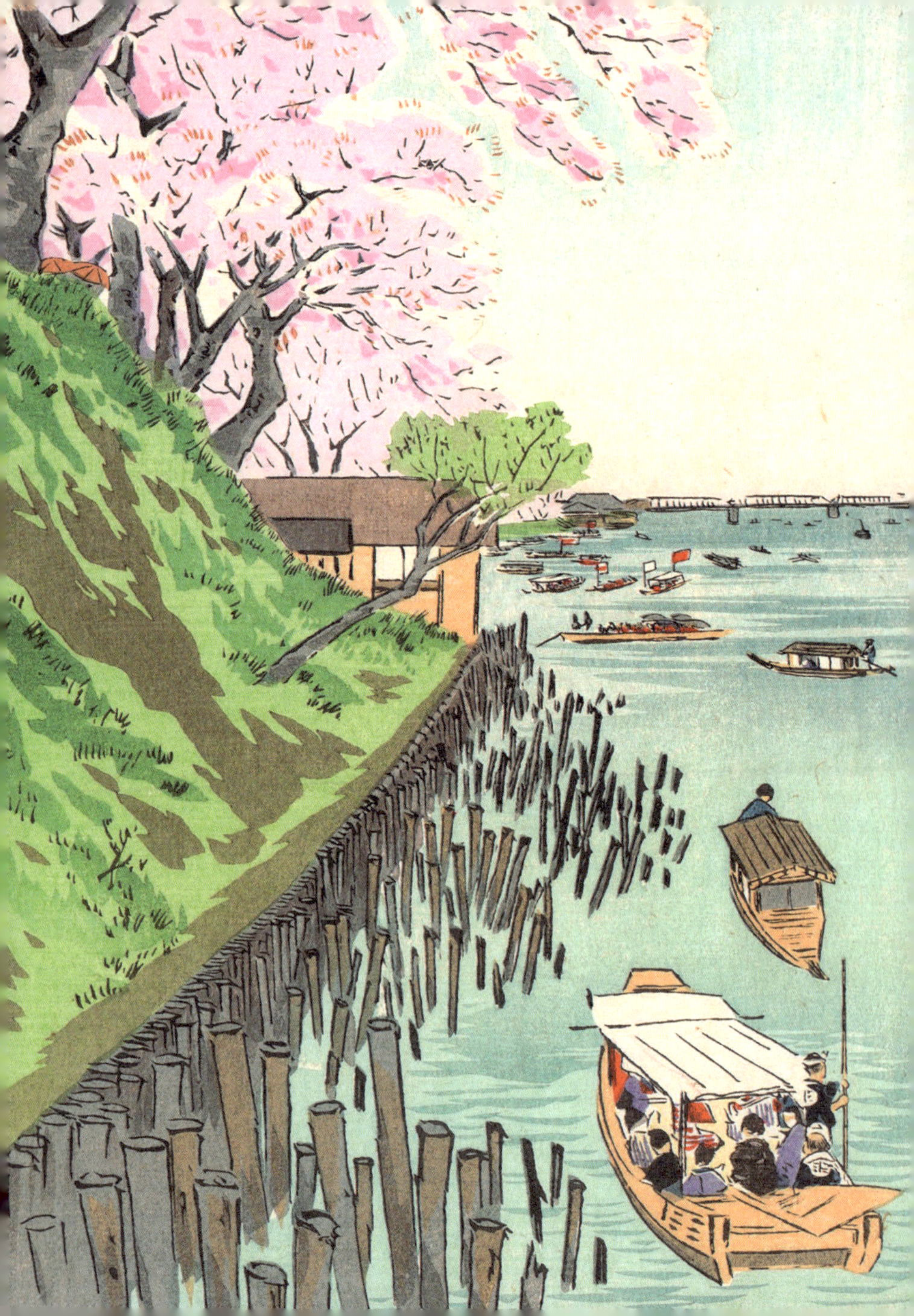

Wabi-sabi

侘び寂び

Find beauty in the imperfect, impermanent and incomplete

Wabi-sabi is the appreciation of nature as the ultimate expression of authenticity. See beauty as it is reflected in nature – imperfect, impermanent and incomplete. This philosophy teaches us that, like nature, we are meant to embrace our imperfections, evolve continuously and let go of the idea of a final destination. Live in harmony with *wabi-sabi* to release limiting beliefs, align with the natural rhythms of life and find peace in the authenticity of your ever-changing journey. What belief is limiting your authentic self – is it the need to be perfect, to stay the same, or to always achieve? Sit with it, then let it go with quiet grace.

NATURE AND IMPERMANENCE

Kachō fūgetsu

花鳥風月

Let nature move and inspire you

This four-character idiom reminds us that nature is both an experience and an expression. *Kachō fūgetsu* speaks to the joy of observing nature's beauty through flowers, birds, wind and the moon. We then, in turn, create and express – whether through art, poetry or the way we live. *Kachō fūgetsu* is more than immersion; it is an invitation to let nature shape our perspective, creativity and way of being. How does the world around you awaken your imagination and creation?

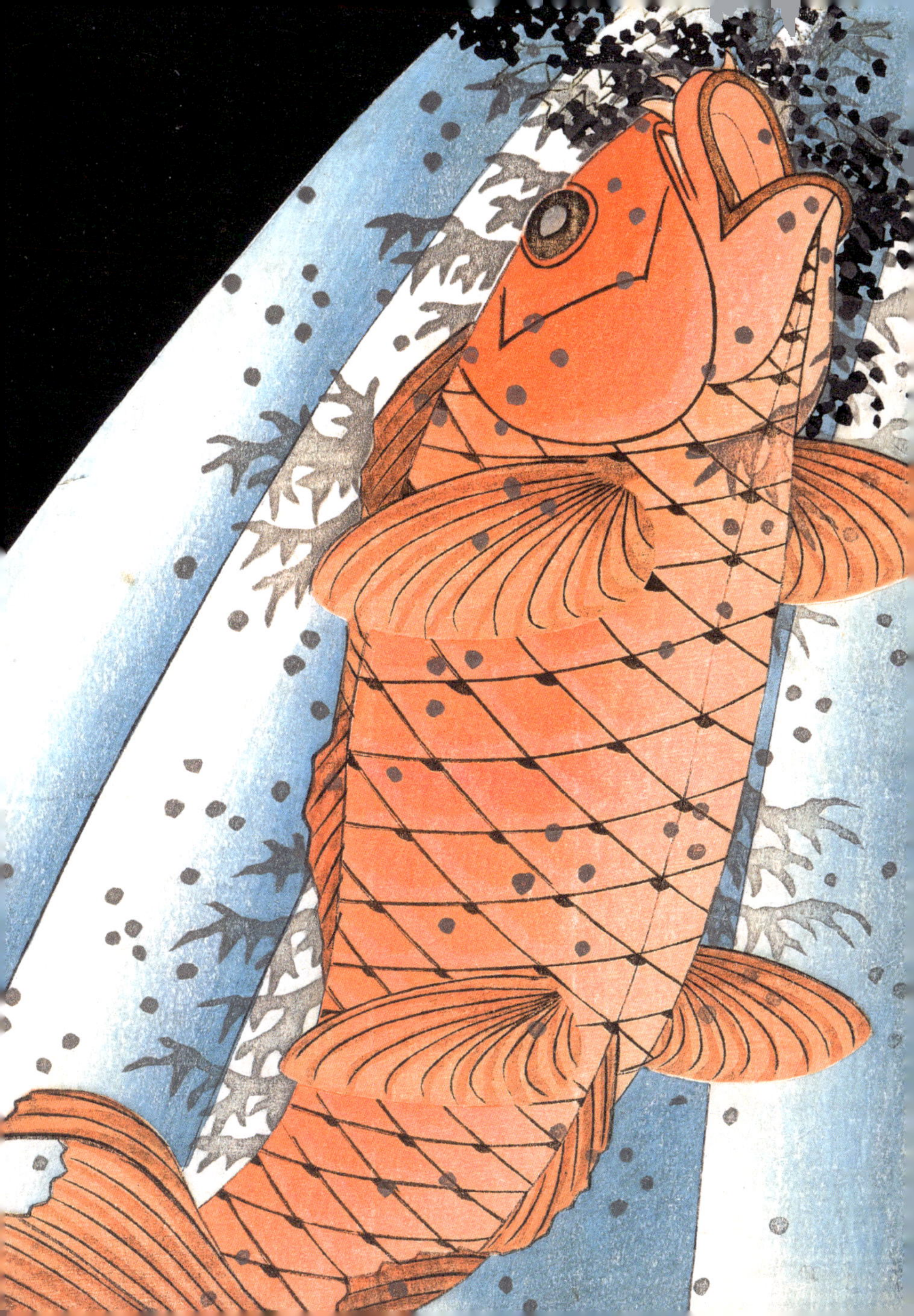

光守教經

春亭画

PRACTICE AND DISCIPLINE

Ittō-ryōdan

一刀両断

Cut through doubt

Ittō-ryōdan, meaning 'cutting decisively with a single stroke', is a principle rooted in Japanese swordsmanship and Zen philosophy. It teaches that clarity comes not from hesitation but from firm, decisive action. Like a swordsman delivering a single clean cut, we must learn to remove doubt, distraction and hesitation with precision. When faced with uncertainty, reflect: what is clouding your judgment? What must we let go of to see the truth clearly? Trust in your ability to act with conviction – clarity is not something to find but something to create.

Kaizen

改善

Continually improve for the better

Kaizen is rooted in the characters 改め (*aratame*, to 'change' or 'renew') and 善 (*zen*, 'goodness'). Together, they capture the belief of constantly striving to make things better. Small, consistent efforts to refine and improve lead to significant growth over time. *Kaizen* fosters an infinite mindset – one of curiosity, adaptability and focus on the ongoing progress rather than a finished outcome. By embracing continuous improvement, we open our eyes to a lifelong journey of learning and development, expanding ourselves to boundless opportunities for growth in every aspect of life. Where in your life can you benefit from a *kaizen* mindset?

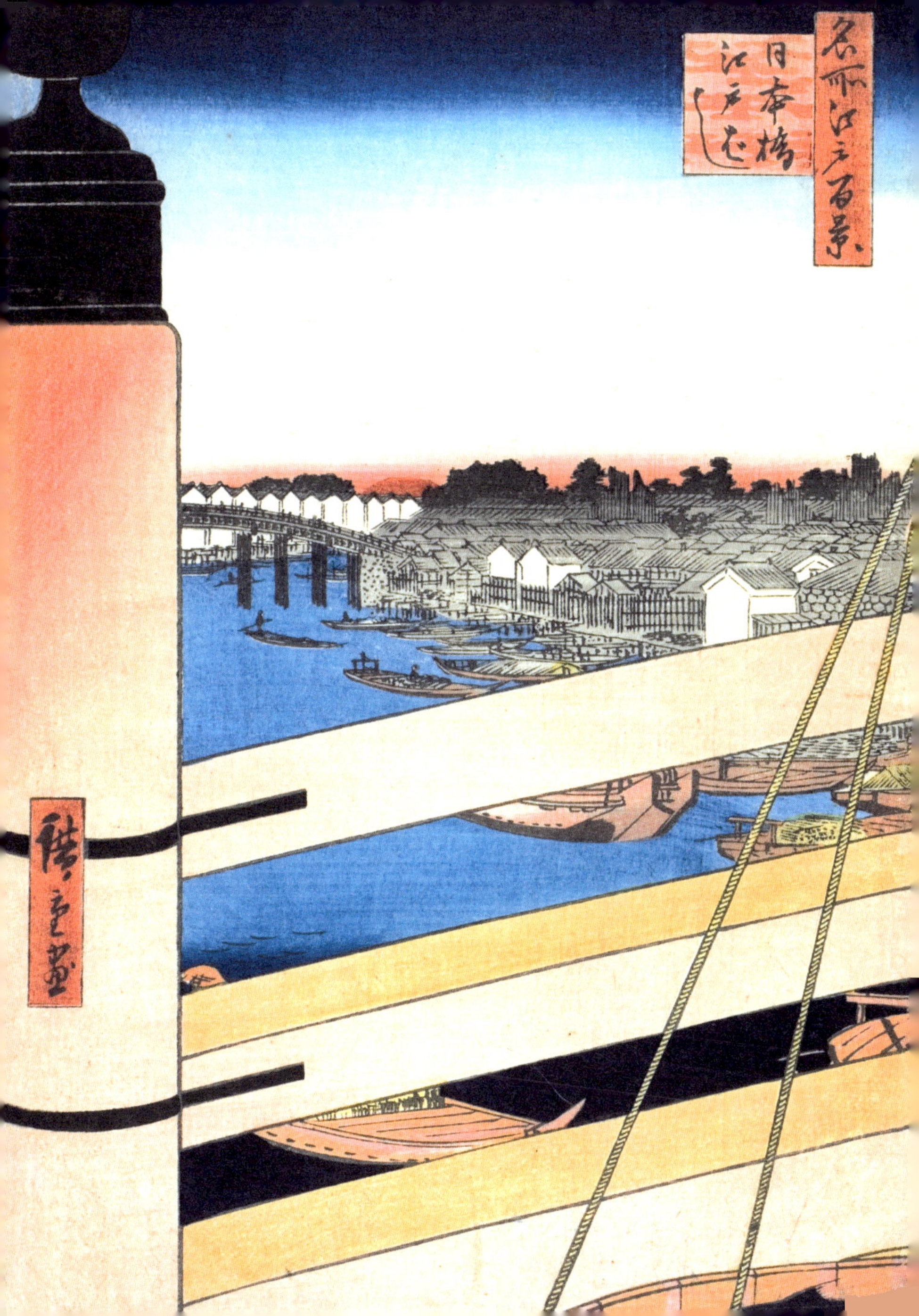
名所江戸百景
日本橋江戸ばし
廣重画

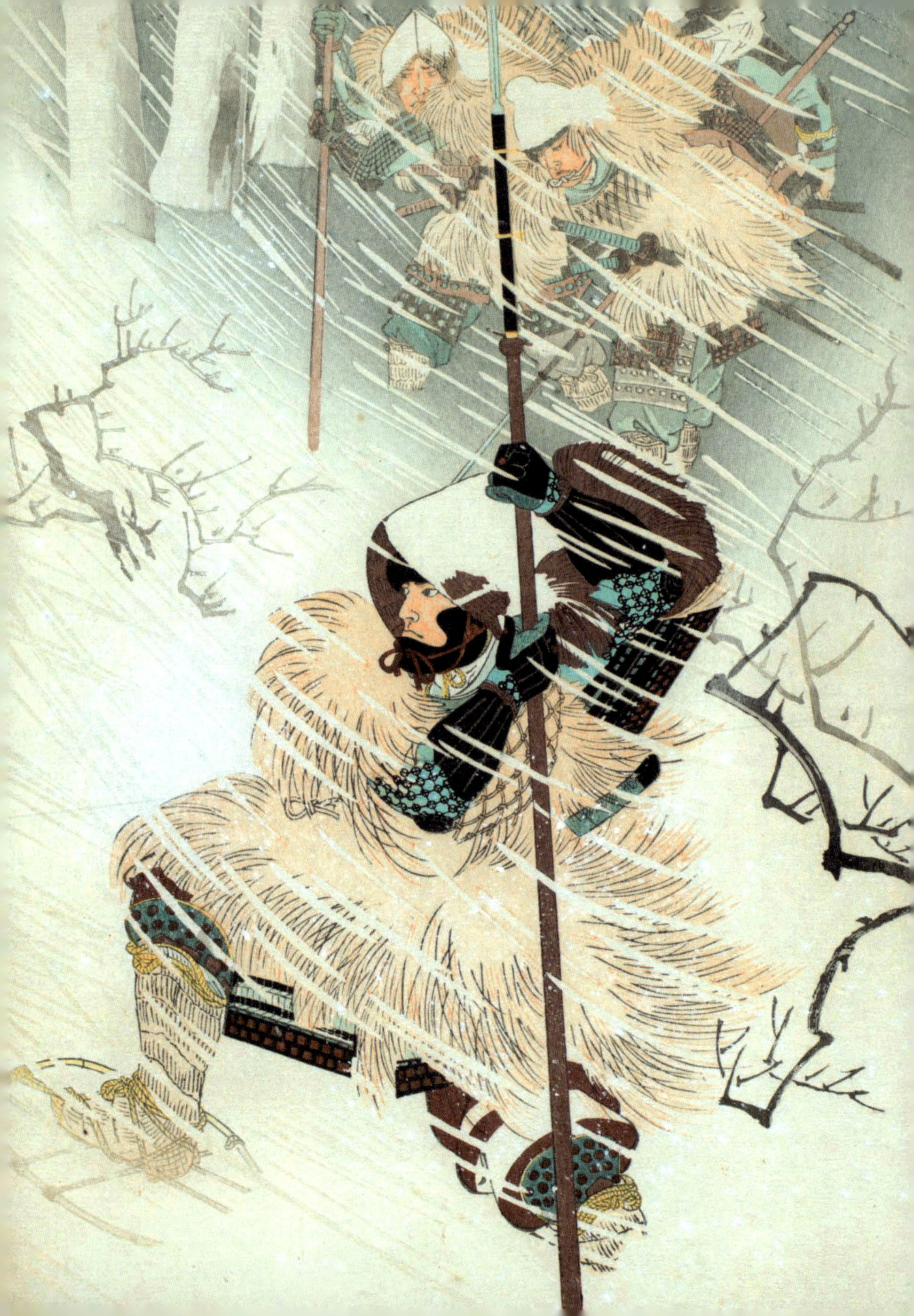

PRACTICE AND DISCIPLINE

Nintai

忍耐

You can persevere

Nintai embodies the wisdom of 忍 (*nin*), where 刃 (*yaiba*, 'blade') meets 心 (*kokoro*, 'heart'), symbolizing the ability to endure life's hardships as if bearing a blade upon the heart – yet remaining steady. Paired with 耐 (*tai*, 'to withstand'), *nintai* teaches us our strength to face challenges. More than passive endurance, it is an active conviction in one's self, where we choose to believe in our capacity to navigate difficulties with grace and inner strength. Let *nintai* give you the confidence to trust your perseverance in moments of adversity.

PRACTICE AND DISCIPLINE

Shoshin

初心

Cultivate a beginner's mind

Shoshin embodies the wisdom of approaching life with openness and humility as if experiencing something for the first time. Mastery is not about knowing everything but maintaining the humility to keep learning. Cultivate *shoshin* by letting go of preconceived notions and ego, allowing curiosity and wonder to guide you. As expertise deepens, preserving a beginner's mind becomes more challenging – this is the true test *shoshin* presents. Let it remind you to approach your expertise with fresh eyes and a sense of discovery.

百人一首之内 崇徳院

朝櫻楼
國芳画

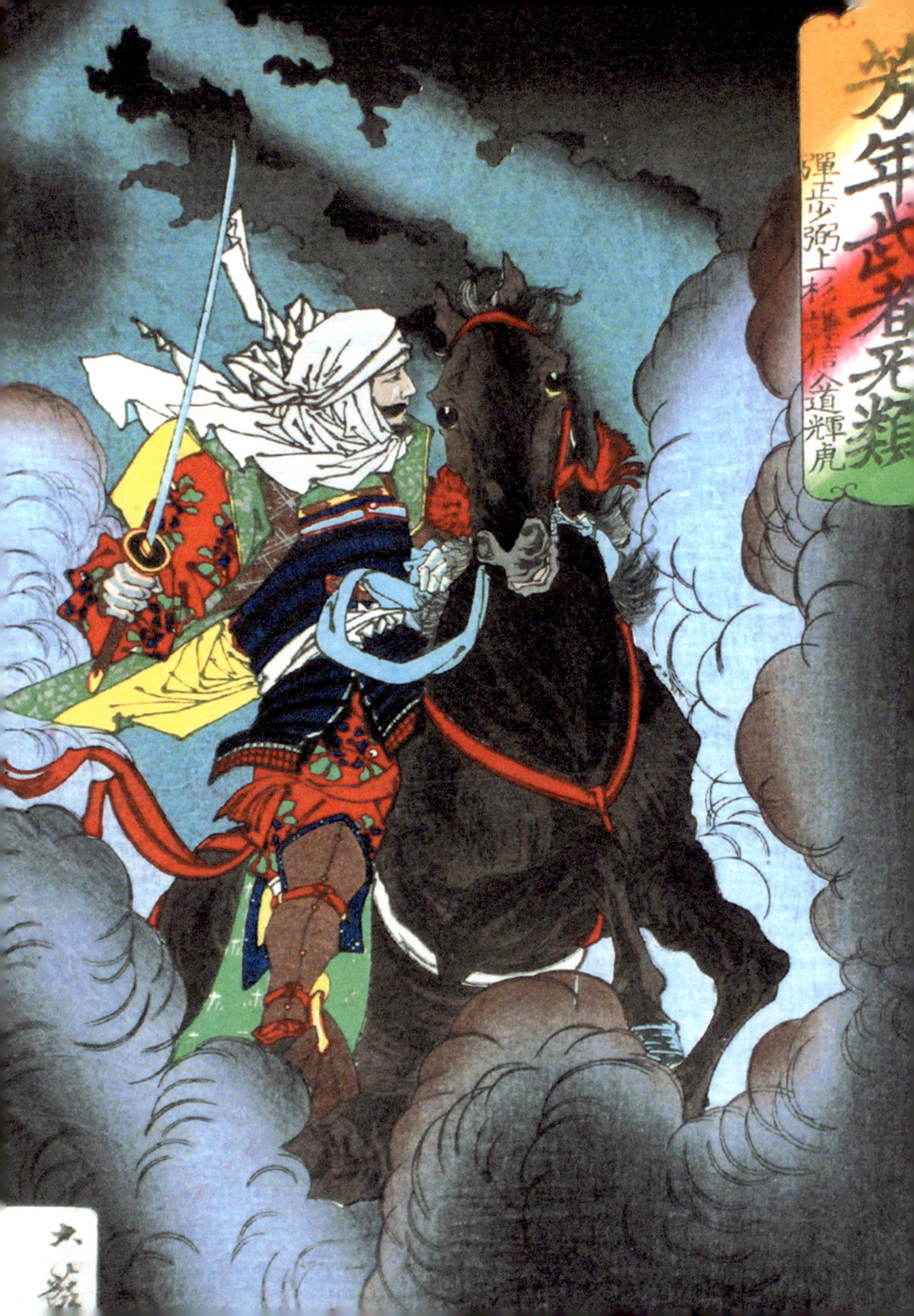
芳年武者无類
彈正少弼上杉謙信入道輝虎

Heijōshin

平常心

Keep a steady mind

Heijōshin is the wisdom of maintaining a calm and composed mind and heart, even in the face of challenge. A core principle in *budō* (Japanese martial arts) teaches us that equilibrium does not come from suppressing emotions but from accepting them without resistance. In Zen, this concept is known as *byōjōshin* – 'a mind as it is' – reminding us that calm is not the absence of doubt or fear but the ability to move through them with steadiness. Let *heijōshin* guide you to cultivate composure, resilience, and unwavering presence in both stillness and adversity. Where can you find steadiness within yourself today?

PRACTICE AND DISCIPLINE

Jū yoku gō o seisu

柔よく剛を制す

Flexibility conquers strength

This principle from *jūdō* (a Japanese martial art) guides us to understand how strength lies not in brute force but in the ability to flow, adapt and apply skill with precision. Mastery comes from knowing how to use energy efficiently, turning resistance into opportunity. Strength without control is ineffective, and the wisdom of *jū yoku gō o seisu* reminds us that fluidity – when guided by intention – can overcome even the most unyielding force. How can you embrace flexibility over force, using wisdom to navigate life's challenges?

新聞 百五十一号

逃げ散らう
人の眼のうちを
浪髪をつかんで
隣の娘を押し
一人を水中へ
とうとう二人を
うちが投れのべ
それと取おさへ
出であるのを
来かかられ
長柄川の
やがて近じ
もとよ
しのぶ其姉よ
楢田六才なるが
本とふる松本
まつ

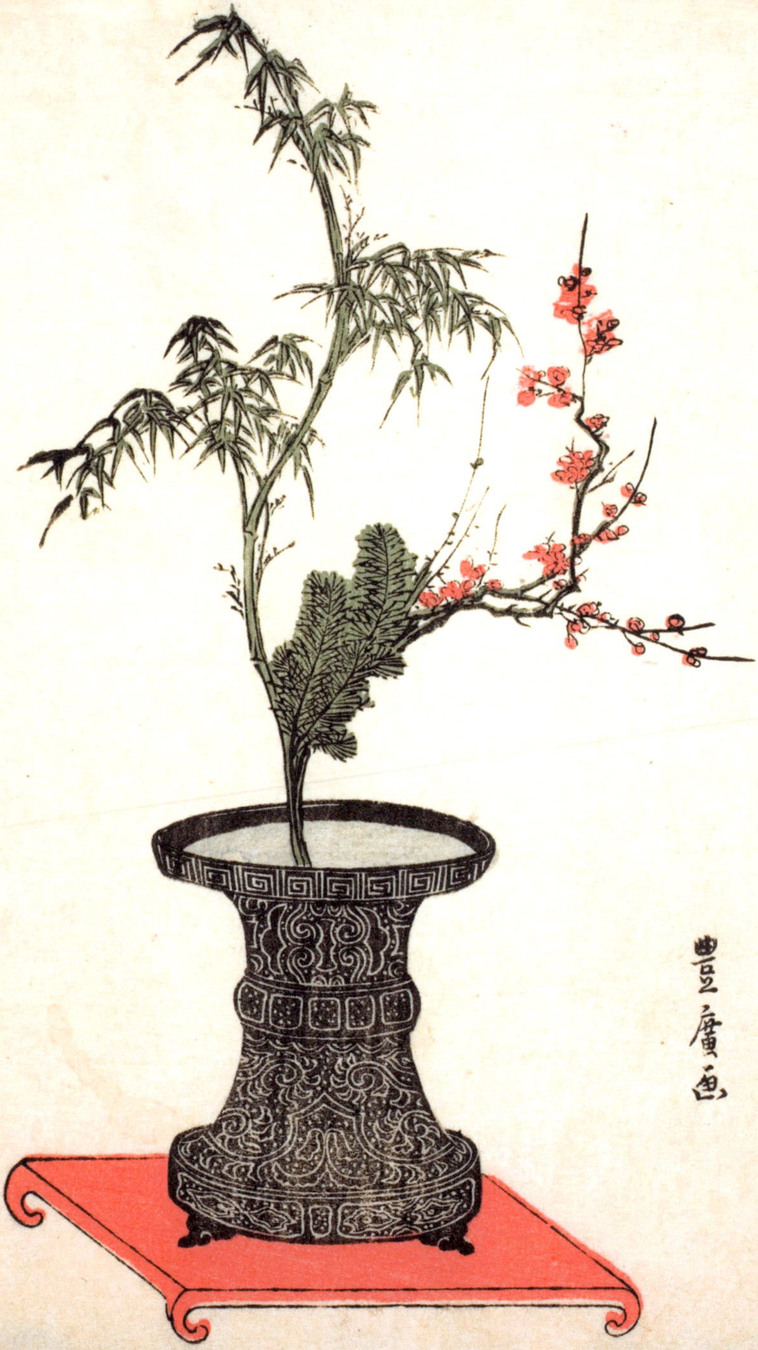
豊廣画

PRACTICE AND DISCIPLINE

Kyojitsu tōbun

虚実等分

Balance the natural and the human touch

A teaching from the Japanese art of *ikebana* (Japanese flower arrangement), *kyojitsu tōbun* embodies the delicate balance between 虚 (*kyo*, 'human intervention') and 実 (*jitsu*, 'natural truth'). Too much human intervention can limit nature's beauty, while too little lacks creation. Mastery lies in knowing when to add a touch and when to let things flow. True artistry emerges when authenticity and intervention exist in harmony, whether in nature, craftsmanship or life itself. By learning to coexist with nature rather than control it, we nurture a genuine sense of beauty in all we create.

Shizentai

自然体

Root yourself in calm readiness

Shizentai is a foundational stance in *jūdō* that symbolizes balance, readiness and ease. Be at your best by moving naturally and without tension, embracing this state of calm readiness. Beyond the physical, align your inner world with this balance – where the mind, body and soul are in flow. Stand in a relaxed, natural stance and close your eyes. Feel the balance of your body. Where can you release tension and return to your natural state of ease? Embodying *shizentai* allows you to cultivate harmony within and navigate challenges with clarity and grace. True strength lies in being centred, natural and at ease.

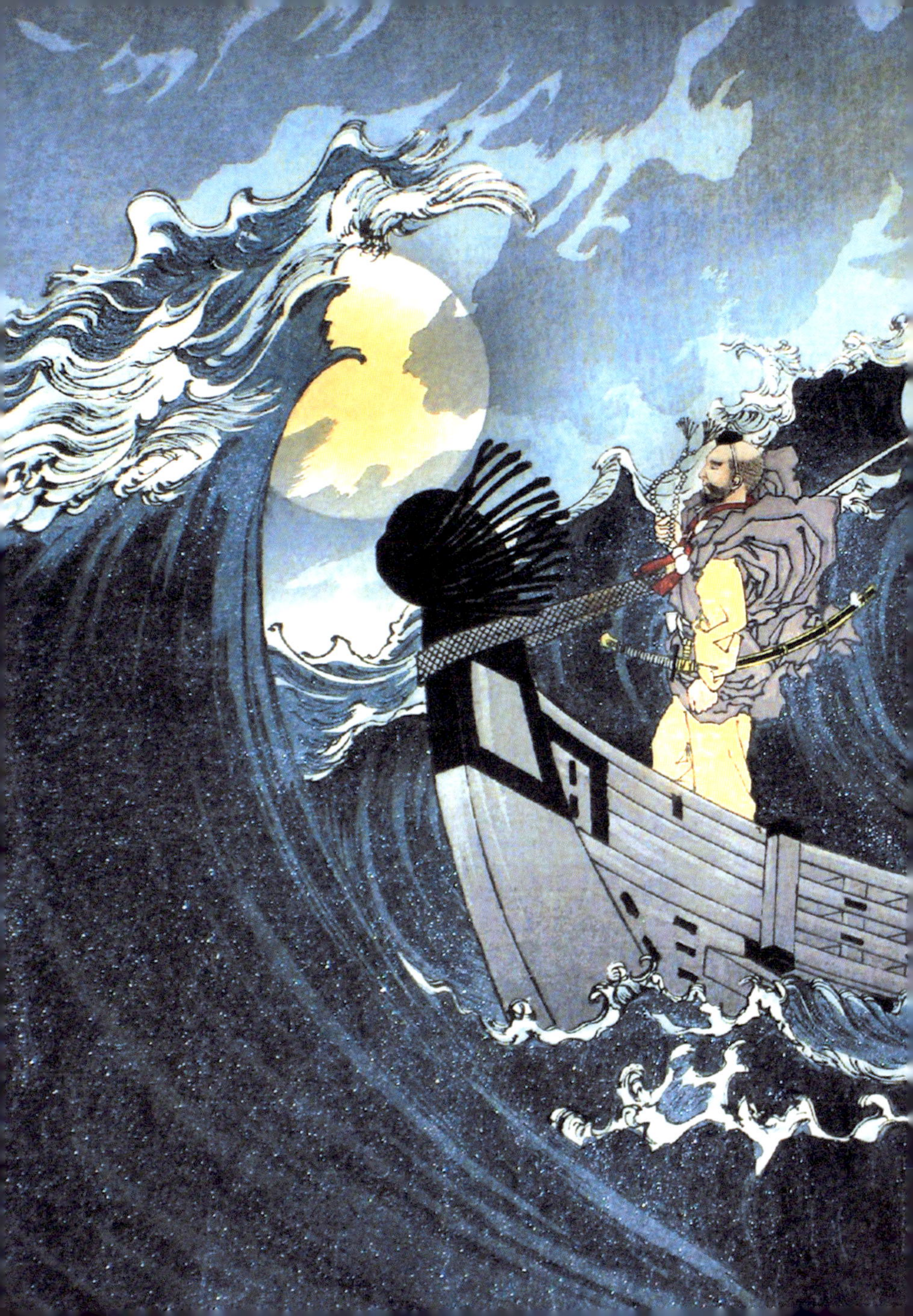

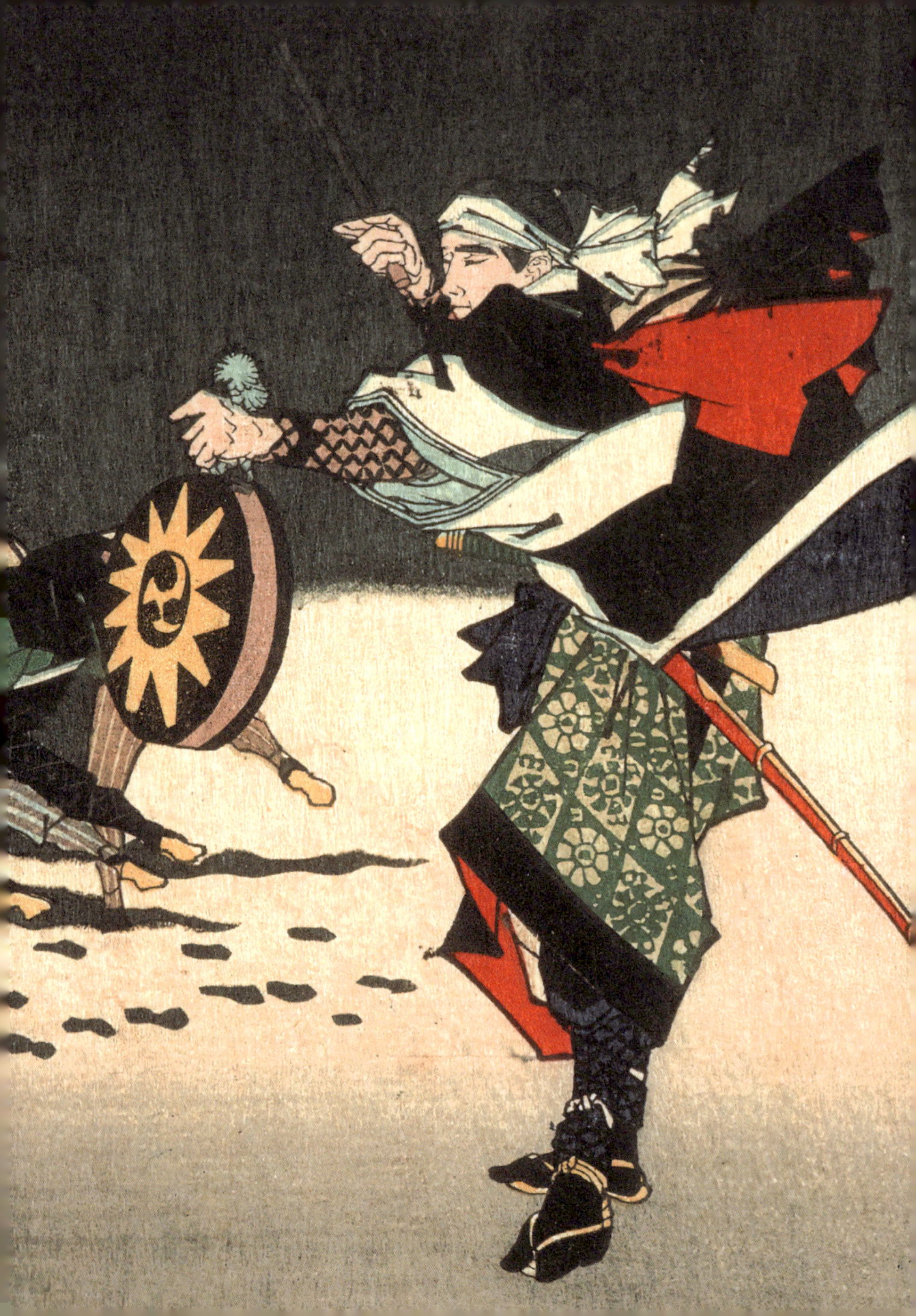

PRACTICE AND DISCIPLINE

Gi

義

Be unwavering in your pursuit of justice and fairness

Considered the most essential virtue for a samurai, *gi* is the foundational principle that demands righteousness without cowardice or deception. It calls for disciplined action guided by reason, transcending calculations of profit or loss, and continuously pursuing what is morally right. Today, this virtue inspires us to embody fairness, urging us to remain true to decisions rooted in justice rather than convenience, and to rise above short-term gain for a deeper sense of integrity. Where in your life are you being called to stand for justice and act with integrity?

PRACTICE AND DISCIPLINE

Yū

勇

Act courageously, inside and out

Yū is the Bushidō (the moral code that the samurai of Japan followed) virtue of courage. For the samurai, courage meant having the strength to face others – no matter how dangerous or unjust their actions might be – to uphold what they believed was right. *Yū* also required a warrior to confront their internal fears and doubts bravely. Genuine courage is never blind aggression or reckless action; it emerges from calm composure and clarity. Consider what courageous step you can take today, grounded in poise and integrity.

猪早太
鵺被刺圖

月耕随筆

稲荷山小鍛冶

Ryūgi

流儀

The art of one's own way

Ryūgi is the unique way or style one moves through life, art or discipline. The characters 流 (*ryū*, 'flow') and 儀 (*gi*, 'ceremony' or 'formality') reflect a refined and intentional approach where tradition and individuality harmonize. In Japanese martial and traditional arts, *ryūgi* embodies the pursuit of mastery through practice, adaptation and dedication. True progress comes from honouring the past while shaping your own path. How can you cultivate your *ryūgi*, allowing tradition and personal expression to flow together in your journey?

PRACTICE AND DISCIPLINE

Kiai

気合い

Channel your balanced energy

Kiai is the concentrated inner energy that brings one's mind, body and soul into complete alignment. The characters themselves reflect their essence – 気 (*ki*, 'energy') and 合い (*ai*, 'joining together') – illustrating the power of uniting inner strength with focus. More than just a battle cry in Japanese martial arts, *kiai* is the embodiment of presence, where energy is directed with precision and purpose. True power does not come from force alone but from the ability to unify and summon inner strength at the right moment. Where in your life can you harness your *kiai* energy with focus and conviction?

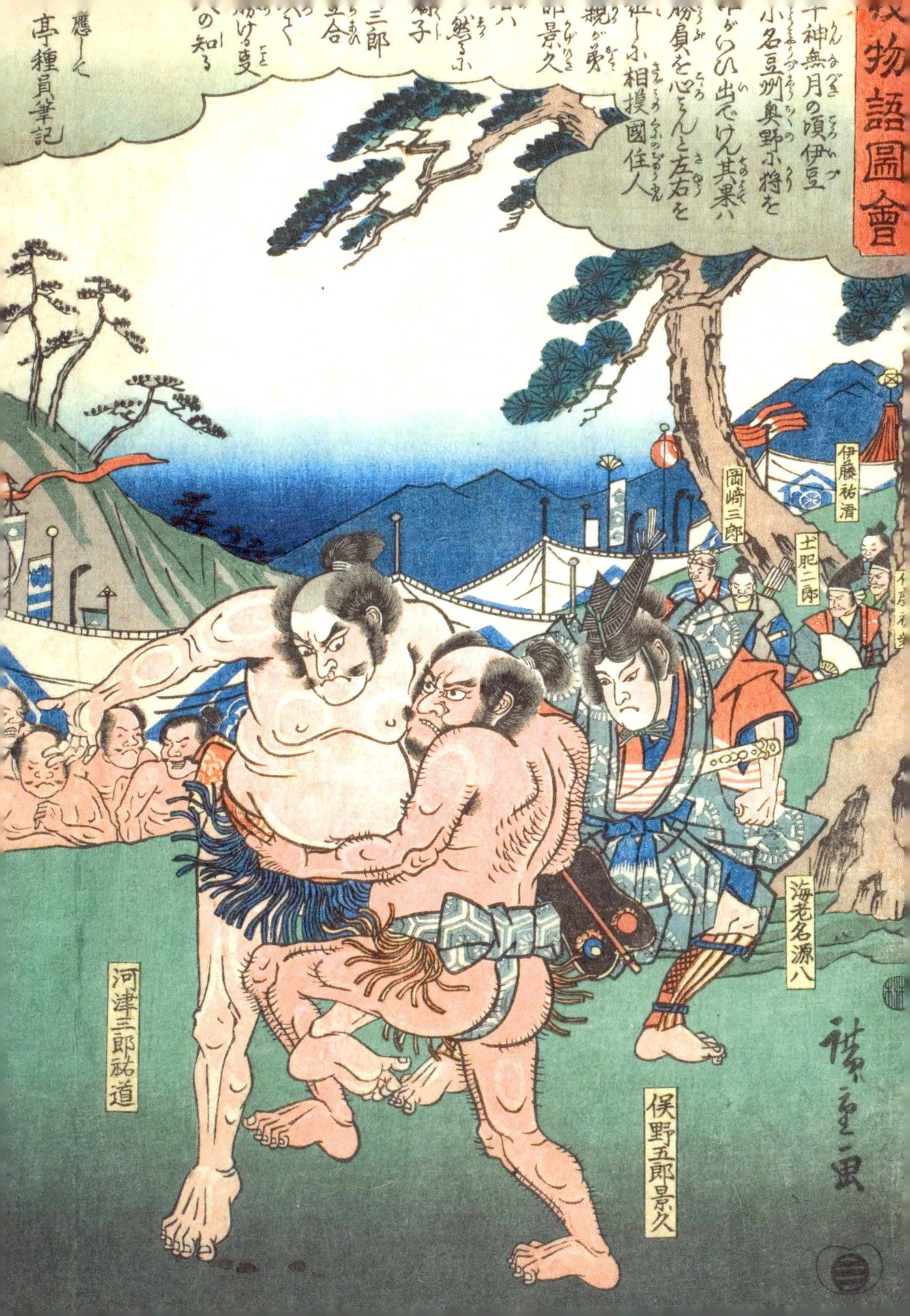

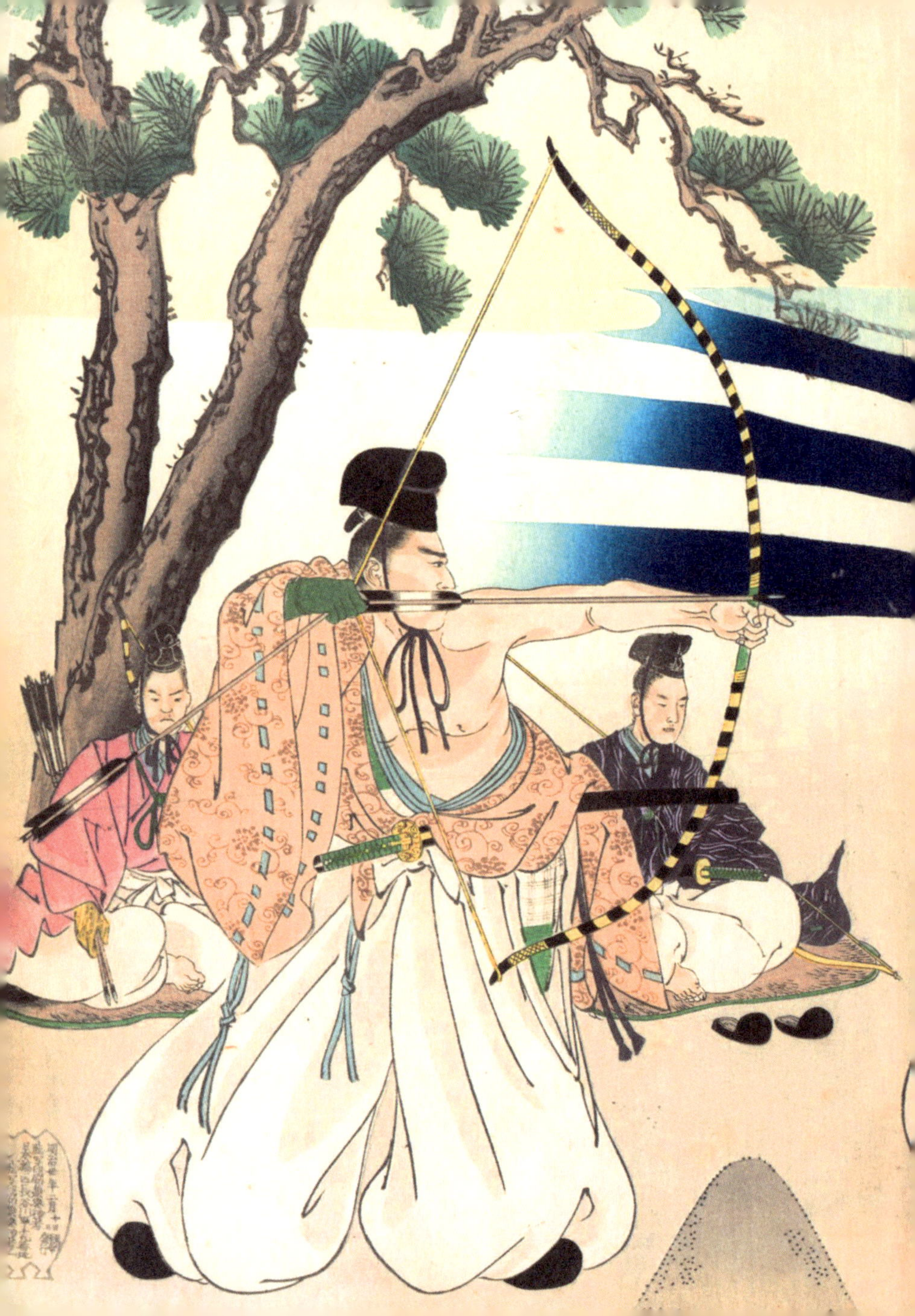

PRACTICE AND DISCIPLINE

Kono ichiya ni sadamubeshi to omoe

この一矢に定むべしと思へ

Focus as if this is your only shot

Kono ichiya ni sadamubeshi to omoe, meaning 'Decide with this single arrow', is a teaching from *kyūdō*, the Japanese martial art of archery. Success is not left to chance but depends on internal preparation, alignment and focus. In archery, as in life, each moment must be met with full presence – as if it were the only opportunity we have. True mastery comes not from hesitation or scattered effort but from wholehearted commitment to the present action. How would you approach your aims if you treated each step as your only shot?

PRACTICE AND DISCIPLINE

Jin

仁

Lead with a kind heart

For the samurai, *jin* was considered the 'virtue of the champion', essential for true leadership. The stronger the warrior, the greater their responsibility to act with kindness and benevolence. While power may tempt one to feel superior or look down on others, *jin* teaches that genuine strength lies in compassion — actions guided by fairness, kindness and understanding. True leaders are defined not by dominance but by the depth of their hearts. Reflect on your own life: where can you lead with benevolence today?

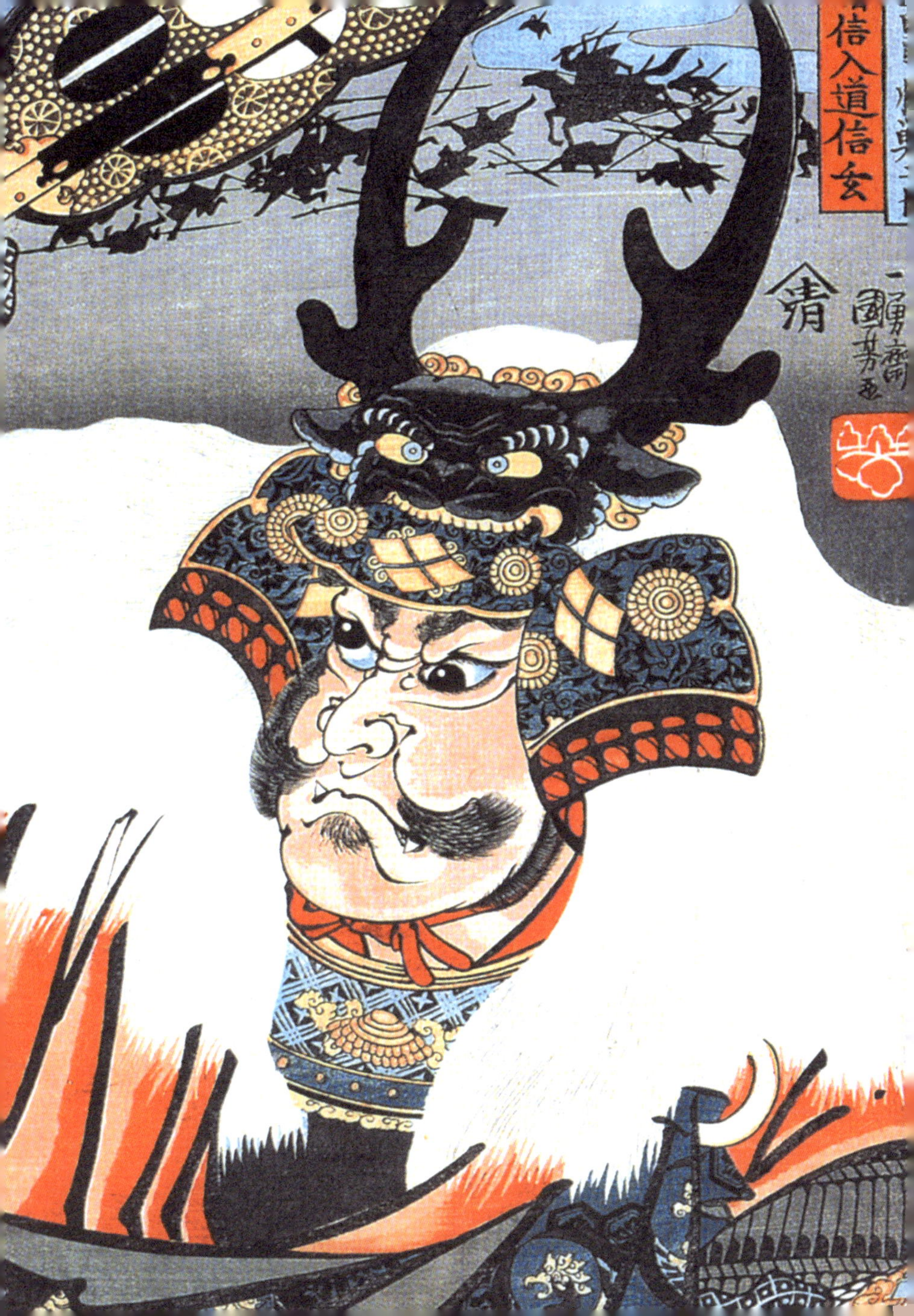
信入道信玄
一勇斎國芳画

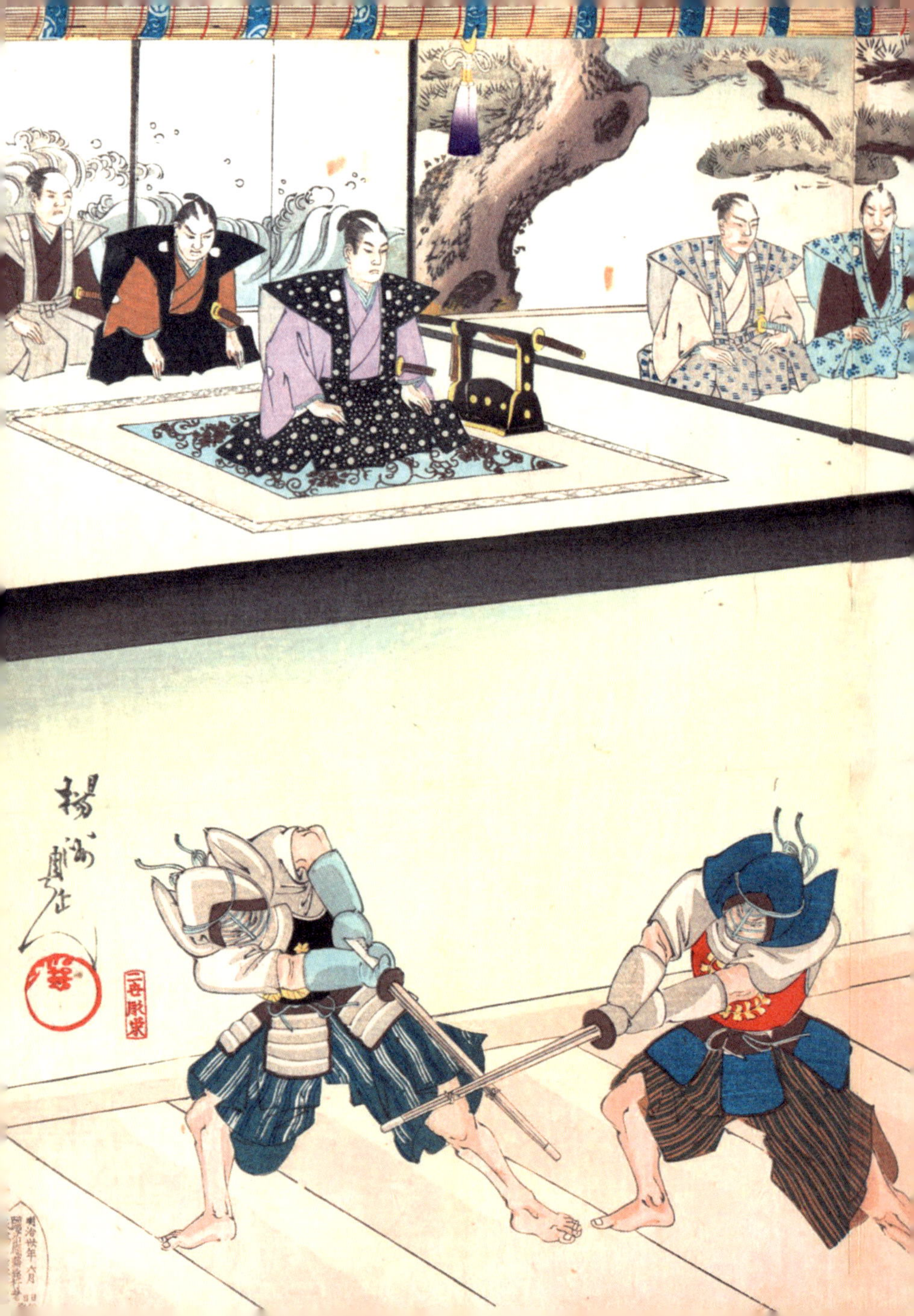
楊洲周延筆

PRACTICE AND DISCIPLINE

Shinki ryoku no icchi

心気力の一致

The unity of heart, energy and strength

A fundamental principle to *kendō*, the Japanese martial art of swordsmanship, *Shinki ryoku no icchi* asks us to harmonize our 心 (*kokoro*, 'heart and mind'), 気 (*ki*, 'energy') and 力 (*chikara*, 'strength'), knowing that true success requires aligning and dedicating effort to all three. This balance teaches us that no single element alone is enough – each must work together with intention. Beyond martial arts, embodying this harmony empowers you to navigate life with focus and resilience, unlocking the strength to face challenges and achieve your fullest potential. Notice how your heart, energy, and physical strength feel today. Before your next task or interaction, pause to align all three with clear and intentional focus.

PRACTICE AND DISCIPLINE

Ichigo ichie

一期一会

One lifetime, one meeting

With roots in the traditional Japanese tea ceremony, *ichigo ichie* is the Japanese idiom that gifts us the wisdom that each encounter is unique and cannot be repeated. When we understand the fleeting nature of our experiences, we can recognize the importance of being present and value each moment as something precious. Are you making the most of each moment or letting your days quietly slip by? Honour this wisdom by deepening your daily interactions and cultivating meaningful connections in your life.

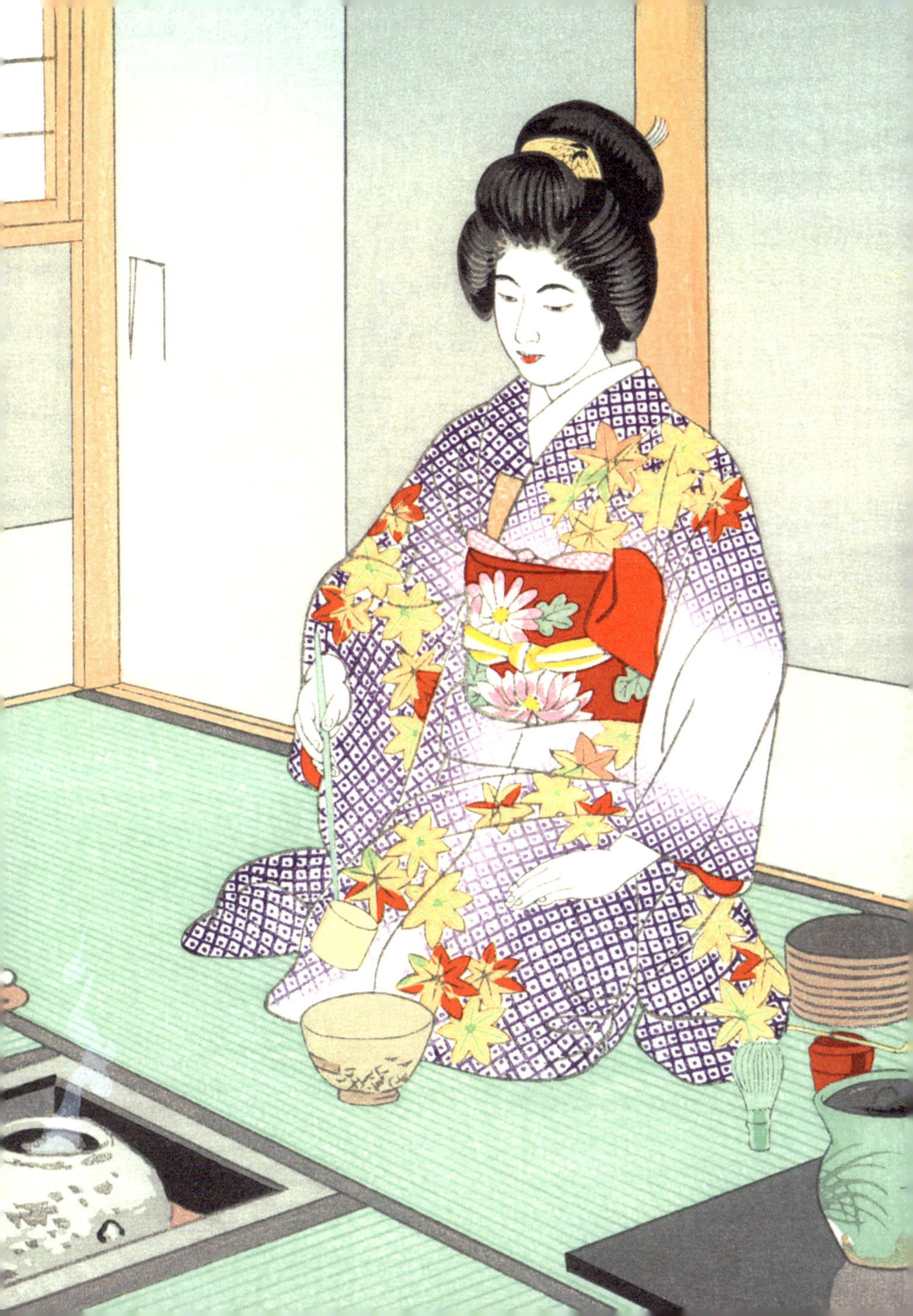

About the Author

Saori Okada is a UKIHCA-registered health coach, Japanese calligraphy artist practising under her gifted name Seisen (星洗), and founder of Mogami 最上 Wellness, a London-based brand rooted in the philosophy and traditions of Japanese wellness. After a fifteen-year struggle with various eating disorders, Saori turned to holistic practices to rebuild her relationship with herself. Today, her work invites others to return to themselves – to find balance, beauty and meaning in the everyday – and to remember that the tools for well-being and harmony already exist within.

Index

A-un
p. 5

Arigatō
p. 13

Chiri mo tsumoreba yama to naru *p. 50*

Daijōbu
p. 25

Genki
p. 10

Gi
p. 109

Go-en
p. 21

Hara hachi bun me *p. 26*

Heijōshin
p. 101

Ibasho
p. 9

Ichigo ichie
p. 122

Ikigai
p. 54

Ishi no ue ni mo sannen *p. 81*

Ishin-denshin *p. 6*

Isogaba maware *p. 46*

Itadakimasu
p. 38

Ittō-ryōdan
p. 93

Jin
p. 118

Jitōmyō
p. 61

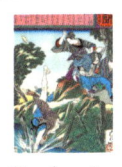

Jū yoku gō o seisu *p. 102*

INDEX

Jūnin-toiro
p. 33

Kachō fūgetsu
p. 90

Kaika
p. 74

Kaizen
p. 94

Keizoku
wa chikara
nari *p. 29*

Kiai
p. 114

Kizuna
p. 17

Kokorozashi
p. 69

Komorebi
p. 86

Kono ichiya ni
sadamubeshi
to omoe *p. 117*

Kotodama
p. 14

Kōun ryūsui
p. 82

Kū
p. 53

Kumo no ue
wa itsumo
hare *p. 78*

Kyojitsu tōbun
p. 105

Ma
p. 30

Mottainai
p. 41

Mujū-shin
p. 58

Mushō-shin
p. 57

Nana korobi
ya oki *p. 42*

INDEX

Nintai p.97	Omotenashi p.22	Ryūgi p.113	Seijaku p.66	Seijitsu p.70
Senri no michi mo ippo kara p.37	Setsunai p.77	Shinki ryoku no icchi p.121	Shinrin-yoku p.85	Shizentai p.106
Shōganai p.34	Shoshin p.98	Tamashī p.62	Tenmei p.73	Wa p.18
Wabi-sabi p.89	Warau kado ni wa fuku kitaru p.49	Yū p.110	Yutori p.45	Zen p.65

Picture Credits

Page 4: Hasegawa Sadanobu I, courtesy of Pictures From History/Universal Images Group • **Page 7:** Ando Hiroshige, courtesy of Heritage Art/Heritage Images • **Page 8:** Utagawa Hiroshige, from the collection of the State Hermitage, St. Petersburg, courtesy of Fine Art Images/Heritage Images • **Page 11:** Utagawa Toyokuni I, courtesy of Fine Art Images/Heritage Images • **Page 12:** Koson Ohara, courtesy of Fine Art Images/Heritage Images • **Page 15:** Kamisaka Sekka, courtesy of Fine Art Images/Heritage Images • **Page 16:** Katsushika Hokusai, courtesy of Barney Burstein/Corbis/VCG • **Page 19:** Ogata Gekkō, courtesy of Sepia Times/Universal Images Group • **Page 20:** Hasegawa Sadanobu I, courtesy of Pictures From History/Universal Images Group • **Page 23:** Chikanobu Yoshu, courtesy of Heritage Art/Heritage Images • **Page 24:** Kobayashi Kiyochika, courtesy of Heritage Art/Heritage Images • **Page 27:** Katsukawa Shuncho, courtesy of Heritage Art/Heritage Images • **Page 28:** Kubo Shunman, courtesy of Heritage Art/Heritage Images • **Page 31:** Hasegawa Sadanobu I, courtesy of History/Universal Images Group • **Page 32:** Chikanobu Yoshu, courtesy of Heritage Art/Heritage Images • **Page 35:** Koson Ohara, courtesy of Fine Art Images/Heritage Images • **Page 36:** Ando Hiroshige, courtesy of Heritage Art/Heritage Images • **Page 39:** Katsushika Hokusai, courtesy of VCG Wilson/Corbis • **Page 40:** Ando Hiroshige, courtesy of Heritage Art/Heritage Images • **Page 43:** Katsushika Hokusai, public domain • **Page 44:** Ogata Gekkō, courtesy of Fine Art Images/Heritage Images • Page 47: Ando Hiroshige, courtesy of Heritage Art/Heritage Images • **Page 48:** Tsukioka Yoshitoshi, courtesy of Asian Art & Archaeology, Inc./CORBIS/Corbis • **Page 51:** Ando Hiroshige, courtesy of Buyenlarge • **Page 52:** Ando Hiroshige, courtesy of Heritage Art/Heritage Images • **Page 55:** Utagawa Hiroshige II, courtesy of Heritage Art/Heritage Images • **Page 56:** Tsukioka Yoshitoshi, courtesy of Asian Art & Archaeology, Inc./CORBIS/Corbis • **Page 59:** Ogata Gekkō, courtesy of VCG Wilson/Corbis • **Page 60:** Katsushika Hokusai, courtesy of Heritage Art/Heritage Images • **Page 63:** Ando Hiroshige, courtesy of Heritage Art/Heritage Images • **Page 64:** Hasegawa Sadanobu I, courtesy of Pictures From History/Universal Images Group • **Page 67:** Katsushika Hokusai, courtesy of GraphicaArtis • **Page 68:** Utagawa Hiroshige, private collection • **Page 71:** Ogata Gekkō, courtesy of Pictures of History/Universal Images Group • **Page 72:** Kobayashi Kiyochika, courtesy of Heritage Art/Heritage Images • **Page 75:** Ando Hiroshige, courtesy of Heritage Art/Heritage Images • **Page 76:** Ando Hiroshige, courtesy of Ashmolean Museum of Art and Archaeology/Heritage Images • **Page 79:** Ando Hiroshige, courtesy of Pictures From History/Universal Images Group • **Page 80:** Kobayashi Kiyochika, courtesy of Heritage Art/Heritage Images • **Page 83:** Suzuki Harunobu, courtesy of Barney Burstein/Corbis/VCG • **Page 84:** Ando Hiroshige, courtesy of Heritage Art/Heritage Images • **Page 87:** Yashima Gakutei, courtesy of Heritage Art/Heritage Images • **Page 88:** Kobayashi Kiyochika, courtesy of Heritage Art/Heritage Images • **Page 91:** Yashima Gakutei, courtesy of Heritage Art/Heritage Images • **Page 92:** Shuntei Katsukawa, courtesy of Universal History Archive • **Page 95:** Ando Hiroshige, courtesy of Heritage Art/Heritage Images • **Page 96:** Chikanobu Yoshu, courtesy of Heritage Art/Heritage Images • **Page 99:** Utagawa Kuniyoshi, courtesy of Universal History Archive • **Page 100:** Tsukioka Yoshitoshi, courtesy of Pictures From History/Universal Images Group • **Page 103:** Tsukioka Yoshitoshi, courtesy of Heritage Art/Heritage Images • **Page 104:** Utagawa Toyohiro, courtesy of Heritage Art/Heritage Images • **Page 107:** Tsukioka Yoshitoshi, courtesy of Pictures From History/Universal Images Group • **Page 108:** Tsukioka Yoshitoshi, courtesy of Heritage Art/Heritage Images • **Page 111:** Tsukioka Yoshitoshi, courtesy of Pictures From History/Universal Images Group • **Page 112:** Ogata Gekkō, courtesy of Pictures From History/Universal Images Group • **Page 115:** Ando Hiroshige, courtesy of Heritage Art/Heritage Images • **Page 116:** Chikanobu Yoshu, courtesy of Heritage Art/Heritage Images • **Page 119:** Utagawa Kuniyoshi, courtesy of Pictures From History/Universal Images Group • **Page 120:** Chikanobu Yoshu, courtesy of Heritage Art/Heritage Images • **Page 123:** Kasamatsu Shiro, public domain

All images sourced from Getty Images